# Men Who Knit
## & the dogs who love them

# Men Who Knit
## & the dogs who love them

30 Great-Looking
Designs for Man
& His Best Friend

Annie Modesitt
& Drew Emborsky

LARK BOOKS
A Division of Sterling Publishing Co., Inc.
New York

**Editors:** Linda Kopp, Deborah Morgenthal
**Art Director:** Susan McBride
**Cover Designer:** Barbara Zaretsky
**Technical Consultant:** Donna Druchunas
**Associate Art Director:** Shannon Yokeley
**Art Production Assistant:** Jeff Hamilton
**Editorial Assistance:** Delores Gosnell
**Illustrator:** Orrin Lundgren
**Photographer:** Keith Wright

Library of Congress Cataloging-in-Publication Data

Modesitt, Annie.
  Men who knit & the dogs who love them : 30 great-looking designs for man &
his best friend / Annie Modesitt & Drew Emborsky. -- 1st ed.
      p. cm.
  Includes index.
  ISBN 1-57990-874-8 (hardcover)
  1. Knitting--Patterns. 2. Sweaters. 3. Men's clothing. 4.
Dogs--Equipment and supplies. I. Emborsky, Drew. II. Title.
  TT825.M62 2006
  746.43'20432--dc22

                          2006024930

10 9 8 7 6 5 4 3 2 1

First Edition

Published by Lark Books, A Division of
Sterling Publishing Co., Inc.
387 Park Avenue South, New York, N.Y. 10016

Distributed in Canada by Sterling Publishing,
c/o Canadian Manda Group, 165 Dufferin Street
Toronto, Ontario, Canada M6K 3H6

Distributed in the United Kingdom by GMC Distribution Services,
Castle Place, 166 High Street, Lewes, East Sussex, England BN7 1XU

Distributed in Australia by Capricorn Link (Australia) Pty Ltd.,
P.O. Box 704, Windsor, NSW 2756 Australia

If you have questions or comments about this book, please contact:
Lark Books, 67 Broadway, Asheville, NC 28801, (828) 253-0467

Manufactured in China

ISBN 13: 978-1-57990-874-4
ISBN 10: 1-57990-874-8

For information about custom editions, special sales, premium and corporate purchases, please
contact Sterling Special Sales Department at 800-805-5489 or specialsales@sterlingpub.com.

# Contents

# Introduction

Designing pieces for men and dogs—two of my favorite things in the world—was a blast and a dream come true for me! I love men—and I adore dogs, too. My own current pooch, Atticus The Amazing Black Standard Poodle, is just about the best dog in the world.

I hope that the men and dogs who knit or receive these knitted garments will treasure them, wear them in excellent health, and not chew them up or bury them in the backyard.

### WHERE ARE THE MEN?

Look around any knitting group and you'll see women—lots of women. But the eternal question remains: "Where are all the men?" If you read knitting periodicals, you'll find men…but they're only models. In truth, male knitters are everywhere. Every year more men are picking up sticks and discovering the sense of accomplishment that comes from creating fabric from a piece of string. There is tremendous joy in our humble craft, and you don't have to have two X chromosomes to experience it.

Historically, men have been avid and expert knitters. They populated the first knitting guilds in France in the 14th century; historian Mildred Graves Ryan in her book, *The Complete Encyclopedia of Knitting*, shares the theory that knitting most likely originated with Arabian sailors, spreading the craft from port to port. In many villages in South America, it's still common to see men making the intricate colorwork hats in their own Eastern-inspired knitting style.

One of my strongest influences when I began knitting in 1983 was Kaffe Fasset, so it didn't seem odd when I'd see a man knitting in Central Park or met a male knit designer. My respect for talented male knitters I knew led me to ask: "If almost all of the men I know who knit are quite good, then why don't more men knit?"

I think it's that damned cool factor. Or rather, a misunderstanding of what cool really means.

Cool is being true to your gifts, and telling those who would try to change you to go to hell.

### MEN GOLF, MEN FISH, WHY CAN'T MEN KNIT?

For me, it's easy to see parallels between these activities and knitting. Imagine the ol' YARN & BAIT shop by a lake in Minnesota, men sitting on the dock swapping stories, knitting scarves, and tying flies? (This would be in contrast to the upscale wine bar/yarn shop I intend to open one day, Knit One /Sip Two.)

## Kenny Chua
Houston, Texas

"I like things to be perfect, which is a challenge with knitting. Being very mathematical, determined, and a bit obsessive, I find knitting keeps both my hands and my mind occupied."

The other reason I think more men don't knit is that the "for men" knitting projects you find in magazines and books are, well, not terribly exciting. The conventional wisdom is that men are more conservative in their tastes than women, and there's more than a grain of truth in this. Ask a man what color sweater he'd like and you're most likely to hear, "DARK blue." The more adventurous men may answer, "Gray." (You might hear a "Black" or "Brown," but they're going out on a limb.)

The dilemma is that these simple pieces are generally NOT the most exciting sweaters to work up. And male knitters, like all knitters, love a fun project. In designing the men's sweaters for this book, I've include interesting stitch patterns and striking color combinations that are exciting to work up, but I've tried to make the detail serve the sweater, and not vice versa.

I've met so many male knitters in the past year: passionate knitters who demand a challenge with every project; knitters who will knit on a long car trip, but otherwise can take knitting or leave it alone; and every kind in between. There are new knitters who have a natural expertise, and longtime knitting men who work the same hat pattern 20 times a year and find comfort in the repetition.

My hope is that all knitters—male and female—will be inspired by these patterns. (I admit that I do secretly hope that the more fun patterns will unleash the funky side of a conservative male knitter…a girl can dream, can't she?)

As for the dogs, well, it's nearly impossible to find knitting projects for them that measure up to their status as Man's and Woman's Best Friend. So I felt inspired to create complementary projects for the dogs—sweaters, vests, as well as some doggie beds and toys.

### SO WHAT DO MEN, DOGS, AND SWEATERS HAVE IN COMMON?
Comfort.

Any dog—and most men, for that matter—will seek out comfort over fashion. An easy fitting pullover or cardigan beats a suit and tie hands down. It's a little known fact that the act of pulling a sweater over the head can release the same endorphins one experiences when playing fetch with Rover (not really, but it *should* be true).

Dogs, in their happy-to-be-here way, will wear just about anything you throw on them. Actually, many a shorthaired pooch will appreciate a hand-knit sweater to keep them warm on a cold day. They may not keep it on as long as you'd like, but they'll wear it. Even if they look foolish, they'll keep it on for a bit to make their human happy.

And so far there's been no "Myth of the Dog Sweater" to correspond to the "Curse of the Boyfriend Sweater", whereby the speed with which a guy flees a relationship is in direct proportion to the time it takes his partner to give him a hand-knit sweater. Happily, giving a dog a new pullover generally won't drive him or her out of your life. In fact, giving a dog a hand-knit bed, chewy toy, or leash will generally result in an orgy of tail wagging, so be warned!

Happy knitting, all you cool men out there!

*Annie Modesitt*

**Annie Modesitt**

MEN WHO KNIT

## William Jones
## San Francisco, California

**"I love combining multiple yarns in one project, either to play with texture, or to bounce color around. I like the fact that you can mix strands of color and not get mud."**

*William Jones, retired professor, and new grandfather, enjoys knitting cabled kilt socks and theatrical pieces.*

MEN WHO KNIT

### Darrel Farris
Berkeley, California

**"I knit for the process, as meditation. I smile as I realize how regular and smooth my breathing pattern becomes."**

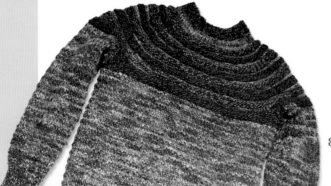

I am asked all the time (by people who are gasping with disbelief that I knit and crochet), "How did you possibly learn?" They wonder, "Was it some sort of genetic mix-up? Did my mom crochet too much when I was breastfeeding?" That would have been a bit tricky since most people need both hands to crochet, and I hope that she would have been more concerned with my falling off her lap than with the doily at hand… But then again, my grandmother had only one arm and raised nine children, and somehow also crocheted. Judging by how all the kids turned out, I doubt there was time to do much more than chase after them, and who knows if there was any breastfeeding at all. I suspect some of them fell off her lap more than once (most likely right on their heads), which would explain a lot.

So naturally, the first question that I asked men who knit was: "How did you learn to knit?" The range of answers was amazing; some learned as children from their grandmothers; some learned from their wives so they could spend more quality time as a couple; some taught themselves; and some don't even remember how or when they learned! The common fiber (ha ha, I couldn't resist) is that they all have intriguing stories to tell. Throughout the book you'll find insightful comments from some of the men who knit.

I hope that the next time you see a man shopping for yarn, you ask him what project he's working on, not whether his wife sent him with a shopping list.

Drew Emborsky

# The Basics

## Tips & Techniques

A few projects in this book are for brand new knitters. The others are for those with more experience. But if you know how to knit and purl, cast on and bind off, and you have completed a few simple projects, you are ready to expand your skills. The following techniques are used on projects in this book. Read them now if you are curious, or look up a technique that is not familiar to you when the need arises.

## Basic Knitting Techniques

These techniques will help you build upon the knowledge you already have and will expand your knitting skills.

### Western, Eastern, and Combination Knitting

There are basically three major styles of knitting: Western, Eastern, and Combination. In truth there could be hundreds of variations on each style, but these three categories nicely summarize the different techniques used around the world.

**Western knitting** is believed to have originated in Western Europe, has become the standard in North America. It is worked with the leading edge of both the knit and the purl stitch

to the front of the needle, and the yarn is wrapped around the right-hand needle from front to back for both knit and purl, as shown in figure 1.

**Eastern knitting,** practiced mostly in Islamic-influenced areas and South America, may be the oldest form of knitting. It resembles nailbinding, a needle craft which uses an eyed needle and a finite length of fiber. Eastern stitches are all twisted (figure 2), which creates a very firm fabric. One form of this style is knit entirely on the purl side.

**Combination knitting** is the method I prefer for straight knitting and purling. This knitting style is also known as Combined Knitting or Eastern Uncrossed. I prefer the name Combination because it reflects the whole-knit attitude embraced by many successful knitters. As the name implies, this style is a combination of the Western and Eastern styles of knitting. Rather than cling ideologically to one form of knitting, mixing methods when necessary is sensible, healthy, and creates a better fabric.

In the Combination Purl, the stitch mount is different from the knit stitch mount. The leading edge is to the front of the needle, as shown in figure 3.

## Using Stitch Markers

I sometimes joke that I keep the stitch marker companies in business, I use them so often! You can purchase all kinds of stitch markers, or make your own from a loop of yarn. One of my favorite resources for stitch markers is the plumbing supply store—the small rubber rings you find there make excellent stitch markers!

Use a stitch marker to separate sections in a sweater, for increasing or decreasing, or to mark points between chart repeats. Slip the marker onto the needle at the desired point, then as you work, simply slip the marker to the right-hand needle before working the stitch immediately following it. Stitch markers should not be knitted into a garment.

## Working from Charts

Working from charts can help you learn to follow your knitting instead of being a slave to line-by-line instructions.

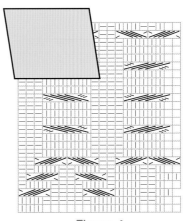

Figure 4

When working off of a chart, place a sticky-note on the row immediately above the row you're currently working, as shown in figure 4. You want to reveal the rows you've knit so you can compare them to the fabric on your needle, so don't cover them up with the sticky-note. You can also use the sticky-note to jot notes about the pattern or chart for quick reference.

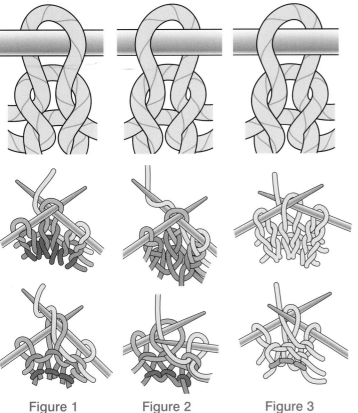

| Figure 1 | Figure 2 | Figure 3 |
|----------|----------|----------|
| WESTERN | EASTERN | COMBINATION |

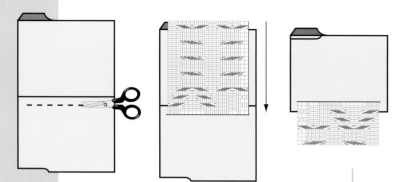

**Figure 5**

When using a very large chart, you can use a file folder to help keep your place. Cut a slit in the file folder and pull the chart out of the slit, row by row as you work up the chart, as shown in figure 5.

## Increasing

Increasing adds stitches to your knitting to make the piece wider. There are many methods to increase, here is the technique I use in this book.

### MAKE ONE (M1), AKA "GRANDMA" INCREASE

**1.** Insert needle into the stitch below the next stitch on the left-hand needle (either knit-wise or purl-wise, depending on the stitch).

**2.** Pull a loop of yarn through, creating a stitch, then work the stitch immediately above (the next stitch to be worked on the left-hand needle).

**3.** Slip the stitch off the left-hand needle.

## Decreasing

Decreasing removes stitches from your knitting to make the piece narrower. Here are the techniques I use in this book.

### VERTICAL DOUBLE DECREASE (VDD)

This decrease removes 2 stitches at a time.

Sl 2 sts as if to work k2tog, k1, pass slipped sts over (decrease 2 sts).

### RIGHT SLANTING DECREASE

This decrease is called knit 2 together (k2tog) in Western knitting, but I prefer to call it knit 2 together right slanting (k2tog-RS). The resulting decrease slants toward the right.

**1.** Insert the needle through two loops on the left needle at once, inserting the needle into the 2nd st on the LH needle, then into the first st (closest to the point). The RH needle will point to the right when working this decrease. Combination knitters need to turn these stitches around so they are "facing" in the opposite direction.

**2.** Work the 2 stitches together as a regular knit stitch.

### LEFT SLANTING DECREASE

This decrease can be called slip, slip, knit (ssk). I prefer to call it knit 2 together left slanting (k2tog-LS). The resulting decrease slants toward the left.

**1.** Slip the next two stitches one at a time to the right needle as if to knit.

**2.** Insert the left needle into the front of the stitches, and knit the two stitches together through the back loops with the right needle. Combination knitters have this one easy—simply insert the RH needle into the first, then second stitch on the LH needle, and knit them together. The point of the RH needle will point to the left during this decrease.

## Picking Up Stitches

Quite often it's necessary to pick up stitches along sweater fronts, necklines, or other edges to finish a garment or add a sleeve, collar, or placket. The terms *pick up* and *pick up and knit* have practically become interchangeable, but they actually do mean different things!

**Pick up** describes the action of inserting a needle into the knit fabric and slipping a loop of yarn from the garment onto the needle.

**Pick up and knit** describes the action of inserting a needle into the knit fabric and, using a separate strand of yarn, pulling a loop through the fabric to create a knit stitch.

**To pick up and knit stitches:**

**1.** Insert needle into next stitch at the edge of the fabric, stabbing all the way from the right side to the wrong side of the work. Wrap a loop around the needle, pull the loop through, creating a knit stitch.

**2.** Pull up a loop in the second stitch using the yarn tail (the strand not attached to the ball).

**3.** Continue to work across the edge of the fabric, pulling up all subsequent loops with the live end of the yarn.

**Tip:** Some folks prefer to pick up stitches using a crochet hook and transfer them to a knitting needle.

# Special Techniques

These techniques are a few of my favorites. I've used them on the projects in this book and I find myself coming back to them again and again when I am designing.

## Cable Cast On

The cable cast on creates a firm, decorative edge. My favorite feature of the cable cast on is that you don't have to measure out a long tail.

**1.** Make a slip knot about 4 inches/10 cm from the end of the yarn. This is the first stitch.

**2.** Knit one stitch. Leave the slip knot on the left needle, and place the new stitch back on the left needle as well. You now have two stitches on the left needle and the right needle is empty.

**3.** Insert the right needle *between* the last two stitches on the left needle (figure 6), and wrap the yarn as if to knit.

**4.** Pull the yarn through, as shown in figure 7.

**5.** Place the new stitch back on the left needle, as shown in figure 8.

Repeat steps 3 through 5 for the required number of stitches.

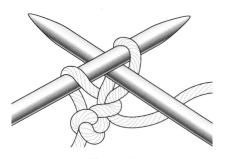

Figure 6

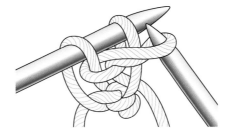

Figure 7

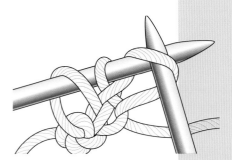

Figure 8

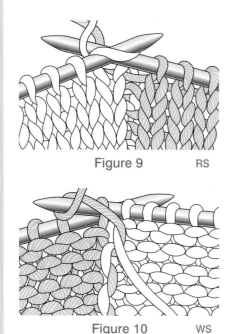

Figure 9          RS

Figure 10          WS

## Intarsia Colorwork

When working in blocks of color, it's vital that as you move from one color block to the next, you allow the strands to cross each other, creating a small twist. This will prevent a hole from forming between color blocks. (See figures 9 and 10.)

## Double Knitting

Double knitting creates a fabric that has two layers. Both layers are the right side of the knitting, and the wrong side is hidden between the two layers.

The concept behind double knitting is that your stitches are divided into 2 groups: side A and side B of the work. All of the stitches are arranged on one straight needle, 1 stitch from side A, 1 stitch from side B, until all stitches are placed on the needle.

### SINGLE STRAND DOUBLE KNITTING IN REVERSE STOCKINETTE STITCH

This double knitting technique results in a fabric that has the knit stitches facing the inside, the purl stitches facing the outside of the tube. Work this as follows with an even number of stitches:

**Row 1:** (P1, with yarn toward you sl 1) rep to end of row, ending with sl 1, turn work.

**Repeat row 1** until the work is the desired length.

### SINGLE STRAND DOUBLE KNITTING IN ST ST

This trickier technique results in a fabric with the purl surface on the inside and the knit surface on the outside of the tube. You will knit all of the stitches that are connected to the side of the work facing you, and slip all stitches connected to the side of the fabric away from you. If Side A is facing you, and the first stitch on the needle is a stitch from Side A, you work as follows with an even number of stitches:

**Row 1:** (K1, bring your yarn toward you, sl 1, move your yarn to the back) rep to end of row, end by bringing the yarn toward you and slipping 1 st, turn.

**Repeat row 1** for the opposite side, and keep repeating the row until desired length is achieved.

### TWO COLOR DOUBLE KNITTING

Double knitting can also be worked with two strands of yarn in different colors. Holding both yarns in the left hand, as shown in figure 11, makes the yarns easy to manage.

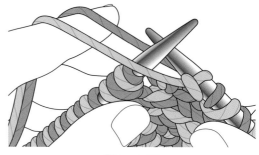

Figure 11

Divide an even number of stitches into 2 groups (side A and side B of the work). Arrange all stitches on one straight needle, (1 stitch from side A, 1 stitch from side B), until all stitches are placed on the needle. If Side A is facing you, and the first stitch on the needle is a stitch from Side A, you work as follows:

**Row 1:** Holding the yarn for side B to the back of the work and the strand for side A to the front of the work, (with yarn A, p1, with yarn B, k1) rep to end of row, turn work.

**Row 2:** Holding the yarn for side A to the back of the work and the strand for side B to the front of the work, (with yarn B, p1, with yarn A, k1) rep to end of row, turn work.

**Repeat rows 1 and 2** until the piece is the desired length.

It is important that the yarn for side A **stays** on the A side of the work, likewise with the B yarn. If these strands cross or twist, you will join the sides of the work.

There are double knit techniques where these strands are supposed to cross, creating a double thickness fabric. The above techniques are designed to create an open tube.

## Working Short Rows

A short row is made when you knit across part of a row, then turn your work and work back in the opposite direction. Just about every new knitter has done this unintentionally, but it is an excellent technique for shaping garments.

Short rows can be worked in various ways, but one of the simplest methods is the wrap and turn. When this technique is used in a pattern, the instructions use the abbreviation W&T.

**1.** Work the desired number of sts in the row, stop and bring yarn to the front (if it's not already there).

**2.** Slip the next st to the right-hand needle.

**3.** Move the yarn to the back.

**4.** Return the slipped st back to the left-hand needle.

**5.** Turn work and begin working in the opposite direction.

When you return work to the wrapped stitch in a future row in the pattern, be sure to slip the yarn that is wrapped around the stitch up onto the left-hand needle and work it along with the stitch. This will help prevent a hole from developing where the short row ended.

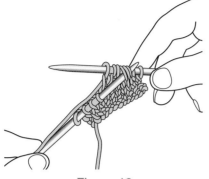

Figure 12

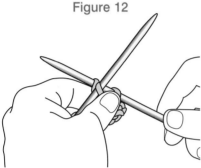

Figure 13

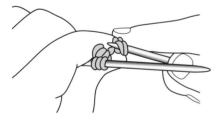

Figure 14

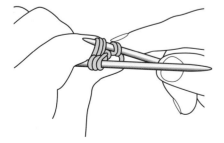

Figure 15

# Cabling Without a Cable Needle

I love working cables, but I find that keeping track of my cable needle can be frustrating, so I learned how to work cables without the extra needle. Give this a try; you might find that you like it, too.

**At the start of the cable:**

**1.** Slip the first half of the stitches to be cabled onto the right-hand needle.

**2.** Knit the second half of the stitches.

**3.** Slide the left-hand needle into the stitches that were originally skipped (see figure 12).

　　• Slip needle in to the front for a left twisting cable.

　　• Slip needle in to the back for a right twisting cable.

**4.** If your needles are not already forming an X, make an X with the needles, as shown in figure 13. (This sounds funny, but it's integral to the success of your cable!)

**5.** Squeeze the knit fabric just *under* the X, carefully slide the right-hand needle out of **all** of the stitches involved in the cable, as shown in figure 14. Keep squeezing, hold tight and you won't lose any stitches!

**6.** The stitches that were knitted will be flapping in the breeze. Slip them onto the right-hand needle, as shown in figure 15.

**7.** Knit the slipped stitches that are now on the left-hand needle and you will have created a beautiful cable needle.

# Choosing a Circular Needle Length

I have never really worried much about circular needle lengths. I choose the longest needle in my collection for most projects and simply pull the excess needle cable out, creating a loop about 20 sts past the current working stitch. It's a method similar to the "Magic Loop" method which has become popular, and I find it a good solution for when working anything but the smallest tubes found.

When working socks, sleeves, or other small tubes, I prefer to use two circular needles in the method popularized by Cat Bordhi, or double-pointed needles for a very small circular area. For this reason I tend to place less emphasis on circular lengths when writing my patterns, which may seem unusual to some knittters.

The traditional rule of thumb for knitting with circulars is to use a needle with a cable length which is smaller than the circumference of the knit garment. If this feels more comfortable to you as a knitter, then this is the way you should work—knitting should be fun and comfortable above all things!

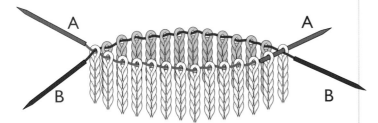

**Figure 16**

# Knitting a Tube with Two Circular Needles

Knitting a tube for socks, sleeves, or other small items has traditionally been worked with four or five double-pointed needles. These can be difficult to manage, and I prefer knitting small tubes using two circular needles instead (see figure 16).

**To work a tube with two circular needles:**

**1.** Divide the total number of stitches to be worked between the 2 circulars.

It is not necessary that the stitches be evenly divided, with half on each needle. You can divide them any way you like, but for this example, let's say you have 60 stitches with 30 on each needle.

**2.** Name the needles A and B. When first learning this technique, it's sometimes helpful to use two entirely different types of needles in the same size, such as one bamboo needle and one metal needle, to keep them separate visually.

**3.** Start knitting sts 1 to 30 on needle A using the far end of needle A to knit those sts, so they stay on needle A.

**4.** Move over to knit sts 31 to 60 on needle B, using the far end of needle B to knit these 30 sts. When you finish with these 30, return back to needle A and work sts 1 to 30 once again.

Repeat step 4 and continue working around in this fashion until the tube is the desired length. End after working sts 31 to 60 on needle B.

It is helpful to move the knitting over a stitch every few rows to avoid a join line that runs down the work between the stitches at the end of the needle. Often a join line can be blocked out, but it's best to avoid it altogether.

# Making I-cord

I'm told the "I" in I-cord stands for idiot, because anyone can make this cord. I prefer to think that it stands for "intelligent" cord. I-cord can be made across any number of sts, but it works best with a total stitch count of 5 or less using 2 double-pointed needles.

**1.** With a double-pointed needle, cast on your stitches.

**2.** Knit the stitches onto another dpn.

**3.** Slip the stitches to the opposite end of the dpn on which they rest.

**4.** Knit the stitches, starting with the stitch above the stitch you started with last time, and pulling the yarn taut across the back of all sts on the needle.

As you work, the cord will develop into the shape of a tube. Repeat steps 3 and 4 for as long as you desire, then knit all the stitches together and pull the yarn through this last loop to tie off the cord.

# Finishing Techniques

These techniques will help you finish your projects with finesse so they look handmade, not homemade.

## Elastic Bind Off

When binding off at the top of a turtleneck or sock top, it's good to use a bind off that has a bit of elasticity. There are several very good techniques, but this is one of my favorites and is quite simple.

**Preparation Round:** (Work 1 st, slip 1 st) rep to end of round.

**Bind-off Round:** Bind off as you normally would using a needle 1 or 2 sizes larger than the needle you used in the project.

## Steeking

Many find working stranded color in the round much easier than working back and forth on straight needles. You can work a sweater as a tube, then later cut apart the armholes and center front (if working on a cardigan). This is called *steeking*.

Some yarns will cling together as you cut, but most knitters prefer to either crochet a chain line on either side of the cut line, or machine-sew a narrow gutter into which you will cut. This helps prevent unraveling and makes the process less scary.

Cut seams can be unsightly, so unless you are felting the garment, or the yarn joins together well (as many Shetland wools will do), you may want to create a knitted seam binding to cover an ugly cut seam line.

## Sewing in a Zipper

To sew in a separating zipper, pin the zipper carefully in place on one side, starting at the bottom. After it's pinned, baste it in place with a contrasting color of sewing thread.

Match the other side of the zipper and pin, then baste that in place so that it matches the first side. If there is any extra zipper at the collar, fold this under the zipper. Once the zipper is folded and secured with a tack stitch, you can cut off the excess zipper.

Hand or machine-sew the basted zipper in place. If machine-sewing, use a very slight zigzag stitch, which will work better with the knit fabric. Choose a color of thread that will blend in with the knit fabric.

This tip was passed along by Helen Griffin and is a wonderful way to make zippers a little less threatening.

Make a chain (of yarn, maybe even double yarn) with a crochet hook, then working with a zigzag stitch, sew the chain onto the teeth side of the zipper tape. Once this is done, using a mattress stitch and yarn, sew the chain attached to the zipper to the sweater front.

In this way only a very small amount of knitted fabric (the chain) has to be machine sewed, the larger portion of the work is done off the machine by hand. It's relatively easy to keep an even tension when machine-sewing the chain. This is a good alternative to a situation where, when machine-sewing knit fabric, the garment can stretch or get caught in the foot, resulting in stretched fronts.

As with any new technique, I use my swatch to test this out using a piece of twill tape. Don't try new tips out on your finished garment—the first time you try a new technique, use your swatch!

## Sewing on Hook-and-Loop Tape

When machine or hand sewing a woven fabric to a knit fabric, pin or baste the woven fabric in place. As you are pinning it, be sure to gently expand the knit fabric to the shape it will take when worn. This will prevent unattractive pulling when the hook-and-loop fastener is sewn in place.

# Sewing Seams

There are several different types of seams used in different situations. The following are my favorites.

## SEAMING ROW TO ROW

This seam is used when weaving side seams.

Lay pieces side to side, right side facing up:

**1.** Pull darning needle from wrong side to right side through center of 1st stitch on edge of right piece.

**2.** Pass needle into 1st stitch on edge of left piece. Move needle tip down on WS of work, bringing it out 2 rows below insertion point.

**3.** Insert needle back into right piece at point where needle came out in step 1. Move needle tip down on WS of work, bringing it out 2 rows below insertion point.

Repeat step 3 on the **left** piece (see figure 17).

Repeat steps 3 and 4 until seam is sewn. Gently pull yarn taut.

**Note:** For bulkier yarns you may want to bring the darning needle out 1 row below insertion point (shown in figure 17).

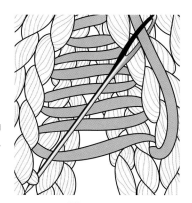

Figure 17

## SEAMING STITCH TO STITCH

This seam is used for weaving shoulder seams.

Lay the two pieces side to side with the RS facing up.

**1.** Pull needle up through center of 1st st in from edge of bottom piece.

**2.** Insert needle between first and second sts in 1st row of top piece.

**3.** Pull needle out between the second and third sts in 1st row of top piece.

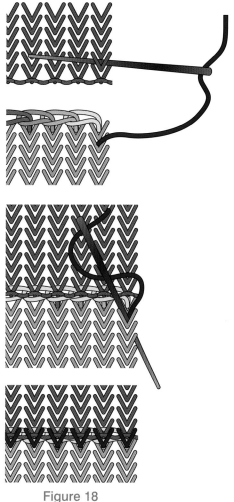

Figure 18

**4.** Insert needle back into bottom piece at point where it originally came out.

Repeat steps 1 to 4, moving 1 stitch over with each repeat until all stitches have been woven together (see figure 18).

## SEAMING ROW TO STITCH

This seam is used when weaving armhole seams.

Lay the two pieces next to each other with the RS facing up:

**1.** Work between sts as per st to st seam.

**2.** Work between rows as in row to row seams.

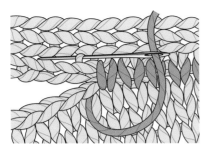

Figure 19

Repeat steps 1 and 2 until the pieces have been sewn together (see figure 19).

Use the stitch gauge to figure out how many stitches per row to sew together. For example, if your gauge is 3 stitches per inch and 4 rows per inch, sew 3 sts for every 4 rows.

## Three-Needle Bind Off

The three-needle bind off is used to join shoulder seams when you don't want to sew them. This technique is also known as binding off together.

**1.** Place the two pieces on knitting needles so the right sides of each piece are facing each other with the needles parallel.

**2.** Insert a third needle one size larger through the leading edge of the first stitch on each needle (knit-wise).

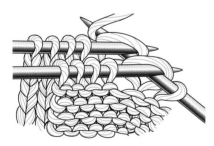

Figure 20

**3.** Knit these stitches together as one, leaving 1 st on the right-hand needle (figure 20).

**4.** Repeat steps 2 and 3 and slip older stitch on the left-hand needle over newer stitch.

Repeat step 4 until all sts are bound off. Cut yarn, pull through last stitch.

# Choosing the Correct Size

## Men's Sizes

The easiest way to select a size for a sweater is to measure a favorite garment. Sometimes this is not possible. The table on page 21 will help you select a size when you are making a sweater for a gift. Use the table as a guide, but measure the recipient for best results (see figure 21).

**Chest size:** The table below shows actual body measurements.

**Chest:** Sweaters should be 4 to 6 inches/10 to 15cm larger than the actual chest measurement for a comfortable fit.

**Back Hip Length:** Men's sweater length usually varies only 1 to 2 inches/2.5 to 5cm from the actual back hip length measurement.

## Dog Sizes

There are no standards for dog sweater sizes. I came up with the following sizes after visiting several dog-sweater websites and checking out books about dogs. I found the same categories (very small, small, etc.) were used roughly for the same breeds, so I compiled all of that information and created the size groups below. Then I visited my friends with dogs, and did a lot of measuring to make sure I had the breeds in the right size groups.

You'll have to measure your dog to select the right size (see figure 22).

**Length:** Measure from the base of the neck to the base of the tail.

**Neck:** Measure around base of neck.

**Girth:** Measure around broadest part of chest.

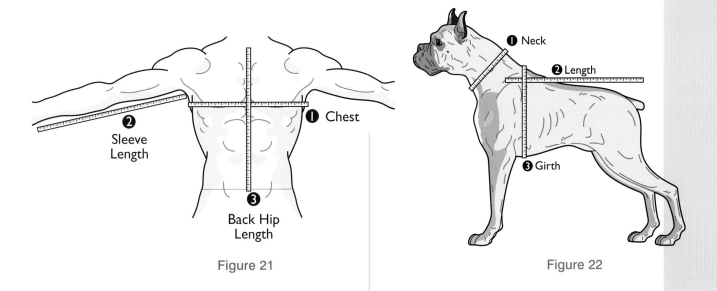

Figure 21                                          Figure 22

## Men's Sweater Sizes

| Size | Measurements in inches/cm | | |
|------|------|------|------|
| | Chest | Back Hip Length | Sleeve Length to Underarm |
| XXS | 30"/76cm | 24"/61cm | 17"/43cm |
| XS | 32"/81.5cm | 24"/61cm | 17"/43cm |
| S | 34–36"/86.5–91.5cm | 25"/63.5cm | 18"/45.5cm |
| M | 38–40"/96.5–101.5cm | 26.5"/67.5cm | 18.5"/47cm |
| L | 42–44"/106.5–112cm | 27"/68.5cm | 19.5"/49.5cm |
| XL | 46–48"/117–122cm | 27.5"/70cm | 20"/51cm |
| XXL | 50–52"/127–132cm | 28.5"/72.5cm | 20.5"/52cm |
| XXXL | 54–58"/137–147.5cm | 28.5"/72.5cm | 21"/53.5cm |
| XXXXL | 60–62"/152.5–157.5cm | 29.5"/73.5cm | 21"/53.5cm |

# Dog Sweater Sizes

| Size | Breeds | Measurements | | |
|------|--------|--------------|---|---|
| | The breeds below are not specific to any size, but may cross several size categories depending on the individual dog | Length | Neck | Girth |
| XXS | Affenpinscher, Brussels Griffon, Poodle Toy, Shih Tzu, Yorkshire Terrier, Maltese, Chihuahua | 7–9"/18–23cm | 6–9"/15–23cm | 9–13"/23–33cm |
| XS | Jack Russell Terrier, Manchester Terrier Toy, Australian Terrier, Miniature Pinscher, Norfolk Terrier, Dachshund Miniature, Silky Terrier, Basenji, Pomeranian | 10–12"/25.5–30.5cm | 9–12"/23–30.5cm | 13–17"/33–43cm |
| S | Cav. King Chas Spaniel, Japanese Chin, Lhasa Apso, Bichon Frise, Boston Terrier, Poodle Miniature, Cairn Terrier, Schnauzer Miniature, Scottish Terrier, Fox Terrier, Welsh Terrier, Dandie Dinmont Terrier, West Highland White Terrier, Beagle, Papillon, Pekingese | 13–15"/33–38cm | 12–15"/30.5–38cm | 17–21"/43–53.5cm |
| M | Lakeland Terrier, Bedlington Terrier, Border Collie, Cocker Spaniel, Sealyham Terrier, Dachshund Standard, Welsh Corgi, American Water Spaniel, Manchester Terrier Standard, Bulldog, Pug, Corgi, Whippet | 16–18"/40.5–45.5cm | 15–18"/38–45.5cm | 21–25"/53.5–63.5cm |
| L | Australian Shepherd, Bull Terrier, Chow Chow, Tibetan Terrier, Wheaten Terrier, Kerry Blue Terrier, Shar-pei, Foxhound | 19–21"/48.5–53.5cm | 18–21"/45.5–53.5cm | 25–29"/63.5–73.5cm |
| XL | Airedale Terrier, American Foxhound, Basset Hound, Schnauzer Standard, Siberian Husky, English Setter, Bloodhound, Boxer, Brittany, Samoyed, Dalmatian | 22–24"/56–61cm | 21–24"/53.5–61cm | 29–33"/73.5–84cm |
| XXL | English Springer Spaniel, Irish Setter, Irish Terrier, Alaskan Malamute, Labrador Retriever, Springer Spaniel, Doberman Pinscher, German Shepherd, Golden Retriever, Akita, Borzoi, Pointer, Rottweiler, Saluki, Collie, Vizsla, Weimaraner, Greyhound, Poodle Standard | 25–27"/63.5–68.5cm | 24–27"/61–68.5cm | 33–37"/84–94cm |
| XXXL | Irish Wolfhound, Alaskan Malamute, Rottweiler, Weimaraner, Greyhound, Great Dane | 28–30"/71–76cm | 27–30"/68.5–76cm | 37–41"/94–104cm |

# Abbreviations and Stitch Glossary

## Basic Pattern Stitches

These basic pattern stitches are used in most of the projects in this book. Every knitter should memorize them.

### GARTER STITCH

**In the round:** Knit 1 round, purl 1 round.

**Back and forth:** Knit every row.

### STOCKINETTE STITCH

**In the round:** Knit every round.

**Back and forth:** Knit 1 row, purl 1 row.

### K2, P2 RIBBING

**In the round, multiple of 4:** (K2, p2) around.

**Back and forth, multiple of 4:** (K2, p2).

Always check the pattern instructions, because there may be additional selvedge stitches at the beginning and end of each row.

### K1, P1 RIBBING

**In the round, multiple of 2:** (K1, p1) around.

**Back and forth, multiple of 2 plus 1:** K1, (p1, k1) around.

Always check the pattern instructions, because there may be additional selvedge stitches at the beginning and end of each row.

| Abbreviations | |
|---|---|
| **Term** | **Definition** |
| beg | begin |
| BO | bind off |
| CC | contrasting color |
| circ | circular needles |
| cn | cable needle |
| CO | cast on |
| dec | decrease |
| DKSS | double-knit slipped stitch |
| dpn | double-pointed needle |
| est | established |
| inc | increase |
| k or K | knit |
| k2tog | knit 2 together |
| k2tog-LS | knit 2 together left slanting, see also ssk |
| k2tog-RS | knit 2 together right slanting, see also k2tog |
| LH | left hand |
| M1 | make one |
| MC | main color |
| p or P | purl |
| patt | pattern |
| pm | place marker |
| rem | remain (ing) |
| RH | right hand |
| RS | right side |
| rnd | round |
| ssk | slip 1, slip 1, knit 2 slipped sts together |
| sl | slip |
| sl st | slipped stitch |
| sm | slip marker |
| st(s) | stitch(es) |
| St st | Stockinette Stitch, Stocking Stitch |
| VDD | vertical double decrease (see page 12) |
| W&T | wrap and turn (see page 15) |
| wyif | with yarn in front |
| wyib | with yarn in back |
| WS | wrong side |
| yo | yarn over |

# Men's Raglan Mock Soy Silk Turtleneck

Have you tried the new soy yarns yet? If not, this sweater is an excuse to do so. Although knitting yarns made from soy are new, Henry Ford had a soy suit in the 1940s. This turtleneck is every bit as classy as Ford's suit!

**SKILL LEVEL**
Easy

**FINISHED MEASUREMENTS**
**Chest:** 35 (38, 41, 45, 48, 51, 58, 61)"/89 (96.5, 104, 114.5, 122, 129.5, 147.5, 155)cm
*See Men's Sizes on page 20 for tips on choosing the correct size.*

## MATERIALS

**Approx total:** 1270 (1588, 1984, 2480, 3100, 3720, 4464, 5356)yd/1156 (1445, 1805, 2257, 2821, 3385, 4062, 4874)m soy/wool blend Aran weight yarn

**Color A:** 369 (461, 576, 720, 900, 1080, 1296, 1555)yd/336 (420, 524, 655, 819, 983, 1179, 1415)m in variegated blues

**Color B:** 369 (461, 576, 720, 900, 1080, 1296, 1555)yd/336 (420, 524, 655, 819, 983, 1179, 1415)m in variegated shades of gray and green

**Color C:** 532 (666, 832, 1040, 1300, 1560, 1872, 2246)yd/484 (606, 757, 946, 1183, 1420, 1704, 2044)m in solid green

**Knitting needles**
4mm (Size 6 U.S.) circular needle at least 29"/74cm long *or size to obtain gauge*

4mm (Size 6 U.S.) circular needle 16"/41cm long for yoke and neckband

4 stitch holders or scrap yarn

4 stitch markers (1 in a contrasting color)

Darning needle for sewing seams and weaving in ends

**GAUGE**
5 sts x 7 rows = 1"/2.5cm in Chart A Basketweave Patt

*Always take time to check your gauge.*

# Instructions

Body is worked in the round to the armholes. Sleeves are worked flat. Body and sleeves are joined at the yoke and worked in one piece to the neck.

## Body

With A and longer circular needle, cast on 176 (192, 208, 224, 240, 256, 288, 304) sts. Work in k2, p2 ribbing for 1"/2.5cm. Join to work in the round, placing a marker to note start of round. Work 2 rounds in Garter St (k1 round, p1 round).

**Set up Chart A Basketweave Patt as follows:**

**Rounds 1 to 4:** (K4, p4) rep to end of round.

**Rounds 5 to 8:** (P4, k4) rep to end of round.

Work in Basketweave Patt as est, following Chart A, until piece measures 7 (7.25, 7.5, 7.75, 8.25, 8.75, 9.25, 9.25)"/18 (18.5, 19, 19.5, 21, 22, 23.5, 23.5)cm from cast-on edge. End after working row 4 or 8.

Work 2 rounds in Garter St, break A.

With B work 2 rounds in Garter St.

Work in Basketweave Patt until piece measures 6 (6, 6.25, 6.5, 7, 7.5, 8, 8.25)"/15 (15, 16, 16.5, 18, 19, 20.5, 21)cm from start of color B. End after working row 4 or 8.

### SHAPE ARMHOLES
Divide work equally into front and back—90 (98, 106, 114, 122, 130, 146, 154) sts each side.

Work back and forth on each piece as follows: BO 4 sts at start of next 2 rows and knit rem sts—82 (90, 98, 106, 114, 122, 138, 146) sts rem. Break B. Slip sts onto holder or separate piece of yarn to work later.

# Sleeves (make 2)
Worked back and forth.

With A and longer circular needles, cast on 34 (34, 42, 42, 46, 46, 50, 50) sts.

## RIBBING
**Next row (WS):** (P2, k2) rep to end of row, end p2.

**Next row (RS):** (K2, p2) rep to end of row, end k2.

Cont in k2, p2 ribbing for 1"/2.5cm, end with a WS row.

**Next 2 rows:** K all sts.

**Set up Basketweave Patt as follows:**

**Rows 1 and 3 (RS):** K1 (k4, p4) rep to last st, k1.

**Rows 2 and 4 (WS):** P1, work in patt to last st, p1.

**Rows 5 and 7 (RS):** P1 (p4, k4) rep to last st, p1.

**Rows 6 and 8 (WS):** K1, work in patt as est to last st, k1.

Continue in Basketweave Patt, following Chart A, AND AT THE SAME TIME inc for sleeves as follows:

Inc 1 st each edge every 6th row 19 (21, 20, 22, 22, 24, 25, 27) times—72 (76, 82, 86, 90, 94, 100, 104) sts.

Work sleeve in color A until piece measures 12.5 (13, 13.25, 13.75, 13.75, 13.75, 13.75, 14.25)"/32 (33, 33.5, 35, 35, 35, 35, 36)cm from cast-on row. End after working row 4 or 8.

**Next 2 rows:** Knit. Break A.

**Next 2 rows:** With B, knit.

Cont increasing and work in Basketweave Pattern as est in B until sleeve measures 18.5 (19, 19.5, 20.25, 20.75, 21.25, 21.75, 22.5)"/47 (48.5, 49.5, 51.5, 52.5, 54, 55, 57) cm from cast-on row.

## ARMHOLE SHAPING
BO 4 sts at start of next 2 rows and knit rem sts—64 (68, 74, 78, 82, 86, 92, 96) sts rem. Break B. Slip sts onto holder or separate piece of yarn to work later.

# Yoke
Worked in the round.

Slip all sts onto longer circular needle, placing marker between each section as follows:

64 (68, 74, 78, 82, 86, 92, 96) sts left sleeve; 82 (90, 98, 106, 114, 122, 138, 146) sts front; 64 (68, 74, 78, 82, 86, 92, 96) sts right sleeve; 82 (90, 98, 106, 114, 122, 138, 146) sts back—292 (316, 344, 368, 392, 416, 460, 484) sts total. Join to knit in the round.

**Note:** Use contrasting marker where left sleeve meets front to note start of round.

Starting at contrasting marker, with C knit one round, then purl one round.

Following Basketweave Patt placement as est in each piece, and ALWAYS working 1 st on either side of each marker as a knit st, work raglan dec as follows:

**Rounds 1 and 2:** (Work to 3 sts before next marker, k2tog-LS, k1, sm, k1, k2tog-RS) rep for each marker.

**Round 3:** Work all sts with no decreasing—16 sts decreased over last 3 rounds.

## NECK SHAPING
**Rep rounds 1 to 3,** while cont in Basketweave Patt as est, until 60 (60, 64, 64, 64, 64, 68, 68) sts rem. Change to shorter circular needle when sts no longer fit comfortably on long needle. W&T.

Work back and forth in short rows as follows.

**Next row (WS):** Working across left sleeve, back and right sleeve sts, cont in Basketweave Patt as est with no decreasing. Stop at marker between right sleeve and front, W&T.

**Next row (RS):** Cont in patt as est, work to point where left sleeve meets back, W&T.

**Next row (WS):** Cont in patt as est, work to point where right sleeve meets back, W&T.

Return to working in the round.

**Next round:** With B k all sts.

**Next round:** P all sts.

**Next round:** Change to k2, p2 ribbing for neckband. Work ribbing for 1"/2.5cm. BO all sts very loosely in ribbing.

## Finishing

Block sweater. Sew sleeve and underarm seams, and sew together ribbing at start of body. Weave in ends.

This sweater was knit with:

South West Trading Company's *Karaoke*, 50% Soy Silk/50% wool, 110 yd/100m, 1.75oz/50g per skein

(A) 3 (4, 5, 6, 8, 9, 11, 14) skeins in color 283 Bluezzz
(B) 3 (4, 5, 6, 8, 9, 11, 14) skeins in color 284 Essence
(C) 4 (6, 7, 9, 11, 14, 17, 20) skeins in color 289 Ivy

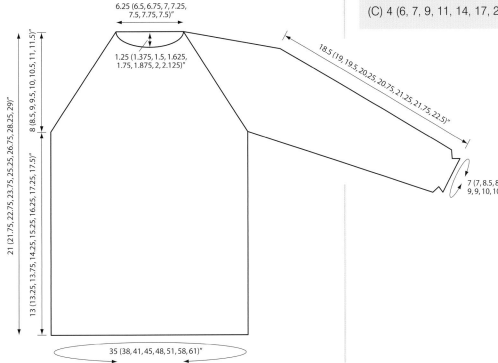

6.25 (6.5, 6.75, 7, 7.25, 7.5, 7.75, 7.5)"

1.25 (1.375, 1.5, 1.625, 1.75, 1.875, 2, 2.125)"

18.5 (19, 19.5, 20.25, 20.75, 21.25, 21.75, 22.5)"

8 (8.5, 9, 9.5, 10, 10.5, 11, 11.5)"

21 (21.75, 22.75, 23.75, 25.25, 26.75, 28.25, 29)"

13 (13.25, 13.75, 14.25, 15.25, 16.25, 17.25, 17.5)"

7 (7, 8.5, 8.5, 9, 9, 10, 10)"

35 (38, 41, 45, 48, 51, 58, 61)"

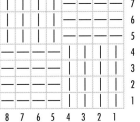

Chart A—Basketweave Patt

8
7
6
5
4
3
2
1

8 7 6 5 4 3 2 1

In the Round:    Back and Forth:

| Knit           | K on RS, P on WS

— Purl            — P on RS, K on WS

27

SKILL LEVEL
Easy

FINISHED
MEASUREMENTS
**Chest:** 12.25 (16.5, 20.5,
24.5, 28.75, 32.75, 37, 41)"/31
(42, 52, 62, 73, 83, 94, 104)cm
*See Dog Sizes on page
20 for tips on choosing the
correct size.*

# Doggie's Soy Silk Sweater

Made from tofu and soybean oil manufacturing waste, this is an eco-friendly fiber. Your doggie friend will be right in style wearing the fiber that is being used by hip clothing designers around the world.

## MATERIALS
**Approx total:** 107 (133, 167, 208, 260, 312, 375, 450)yd/97 (121, 152, 189, 237, 284, 341, 410)m wool blend Aran weight yarn

**Color A:** 37 (46, 58, 72, 90, 108, 130, 156)yd/34 (42, 53, 66, 82, 98, 118, 142)m in variegated blues

**Color B:** 37 (46, 58, 72, 90, 108, 130, 156)yd/34 (42, 53, 66, 82, 98, 118, 142)m in variegated shades of gray and green

**Color C:** 33 (41, 51, 64, 80, 96, 115, 138)yd/30 (37, 46, 58, 73, 87, 105, 126)m in solid green

**Knitting needles**
4.5mm (Size 7 U.S.) circular needle in a length shorter than the sweater chest measurement *or size to obtain gauge*

4mm (Size 6 U.S.) circular needle in a length shorter than the sweater neck measurement, double-pointed needles for smallest sizes

Darning needle for weaving in ends

## GAUGE
3.75 sts and 5 rows = 1"/2.5cm in St st using 4.5mm (Size 7 U.S.) needles

*Always take time to check your gauge.*

# Instructions
Body is worked from the neck to the armholes in the round, then back and chest are worked back and forth. The pieces are rejoined and the waist is worked in the round.

## Body
With smaller needle and B, cast on 24 (32, 40, 48, 56, 64, 72, 80) sts. Join to work in the round.

Work in k2, p2 ribbing for 4 (4, 6, 6, 8, 8, 8, 10) rounds, then switch to A and work 6 more rounds in ribbing. Switch to larger needles and B and cont in St st, inc 1 (3, 0, 2, 4, 1, 3, 0) sts evenly around work—25 (35, 40, 50, 60, 65, 75, 80) sts.

**Round 1:** With C, *k5 (7, 8, 10, 12, 13, 15, 16) sts, YO, place marker, rep from * to end of round, end—30 (40, 45, 55, 65, 70, 80, 85) sts.

**Round 2:** K all sts.

**Round 3:** *Work to marker, YO, slip market rep from * to end of round.

Cont in this manner, inc 5 sts every other round by working a YO before each marker until there are 45 (60, 75, 90, 110, 120, 140, 150) sts. Switch to A and work 2 rounds in Garter St (k1 round, p1 round).

**Next round:** K all sts.

Cont working in St st with no further shaping until piece measures 4.25 (5.5, 7, 8.5, 9.75, 11.25, 12.5, 14)"/11 (14, 18, 21.5, 25, 28.5, 32, 35.5) cm from cast-on edge (or length to fit from dog's neck to arm comfortably).

Purl 1 round.

Remove all markers but one; this will be the dog's center chest.

**Next round:** With C k, dec 0 (0, 0, 1, 2, 0, 2, 1) sts evenly around—45 (60, 75, 89, 108, 120, 138, 149) sts rem.

## CHEST
Worked back and forth.

**Next row (RS):** Switch to smaller needles. Starting at marker k1, work in k2, p2 ribbing, rep until 9 (12, 15, 17, 20, 24, 26, 29) sts have been worked, turn.

**Next row (WS):** Work back to center marker, remove marker and cont in ribbing as est, continue in k2, p2 ribbing for 9 (12, 15, 17, 20, 24, 26, 29) more sts, turn.

You have just worked 18 (24, 30, 34, 40, 48, 52, 58) sts across the center chest. The center 2 sts are knit sts when viewed from the right side.

Cont working with only the center chest sts, work in ribbing as est for 4 (8, 8, 12, 12, 16, 16, 20) rows.

**Next row (RS):** Working only with the center chest sts, k8 (11, 14, 16, 19, 23, 25, 28) sts, k2tog (creating center st), work to end—17 (23, 29, 33, 39, 47, 51, 57) sts rem.

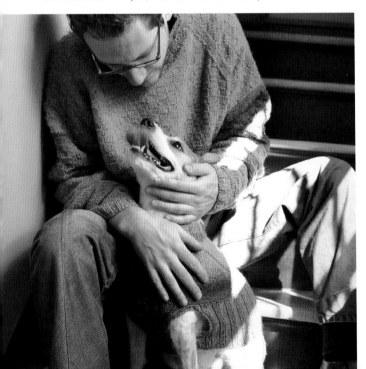

**Next row (WS):** Work even in ribbing as est.

**Next row (RS):** Work in ribbing as est to 1 st before center st, VDD, work to end of center chest sts in ribbing—15 (21, 27, 31, 37, 45, 49, 55) sts rem.

**Next row (WS):** Work even in ribbing as est.

**Next row (RS):** Dec 1 st, work in ribbing as est with no center decrease to last 2 sts, dec 1 st—13 (19, 25, 29, 35, 43, 47, 53) sts rem.

**Repeat last 2 rows** once—11 (17, 23, 27, 33, 41, 45, 51) sts rem.

**Next row (WS):** Working in ribbing as est, k the knit sts, p the purl sts.

**Next row (RS):** Work in ribbing as est to 1 st before center st, VDD, work to end of center chest sts in rib—9 (15, 21, 25, 31, 39, 43, 49) sts rem.

**Repeat last 2 rows** until—9 (9, 11, 11, 17, 19, 21, 23) sts rem across center chest.

Work center chest sts even with no shaping until armhole measures 2.25 (3, 3.75, 4.5, 5.25, 6, 6.75, 7.5)"/5.5 (7.5, 9.5 11.5, 13.5, 15, 17, 19) cm. Break yarn.

## BACK
Reattach yarn to back.

**Next row (RS):** Working with back 36 (48, 60, 72, 88, 96, 112, 120) sts only, k1, (p2, k2) rep to last 3 sts, p2, k1.

Work even in ribbing as est until back is the same length as chest.

# Joining Body After Armhole
Worked in the round.

**Next round (RS):** Work across all back sts, join with center front sts. Work to 1 st before center st, VDD, work to end of center fronts sts, join with back sts—43 (61, 79, 95, 117, 133, 153, 167) sts.

Cont in ribbing around all sts as est. Work even in the round with no further shaping until piece measures 9.25 (12.25, 15.5, 18.75, 21.5, 24.75, 27.75, 31)"/23.5 (31, 39.25, 47.5, 54.5, 63, 70.5, 78.75)cm from cast on, or desired length. BO all sts loosely using larger needle.

# Finishing

Steam block, weave in ends.

## This sweater was knit with:

South West Trading Company's *Karaoke*, 50% Soy Silk/50% wool, 110 yd/100m, 1.75oz/50g per skein

(A) 1 (1, 1, 1, 1, 2, 2, 3)  skein in color 283 Bluezzz

(B) 1 (1, 1, 1, 1, 2, 2, 3)  skein in color 284 Essence

(C) 1 (1, 1, 1, 1, 2, 2, 3)  skein in color 289 Ivy

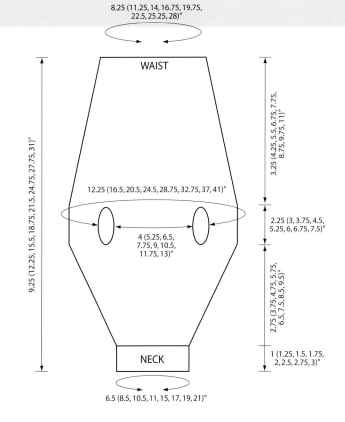

8.25 (11.25, 14, 16.75, 19.75, 22.5, 25.25, 28)"

WAIST

12.25 (16.5, 20.5, 24.5, 28.75, 32.75, 37, 41)"

4 (5.25, 6.5, 7.75, 9, 10.5, 11.75, 13)"

9.25 (12.25, 15.5, 18.75, 21.5, 24.75, 27.75, 31)"

3.25 (4.25, 5.5, 6.75, 7.75, 8.75, 9.75, 11)"

2.25 (3, 3.75, 4.5, 5.25, 6, 6.75, 7.5)"

2.75 (3.75, 4.75, 5.75, 6.5, 7.5, 8.5, 9.5)"

NECK

1 (1.25, 1.5, 1.75, 2, 2.5, 2.75, 3)"

6.5 (8.5, 10.5, 11, 15, 17, 19, 21)"

MEN WHO KNIT

## Lou Simon
Atlanta, Georgia

"I learned to crochet from a neighbor when I was eight years old, and when I couldn't find any crochet patterns for boy's or men's clothing, I bought a how-to-knit book and taught myself."

FINISHED
MEASUREMENTS
38 (42, 46, 50, 54, 58, 62,
66)"/96.5 (106.5, 117, 127,
137, 147.5, 157.5, 167.5)cm
*See Men's Sizes on page
20 for tips on choosing the
correct size.*

# Variegated Yoke Pullover

Made with a silk/wool blend yarn in three variegated colorways, this sweater combines colorwork with garter stripes. The colors are neutral, but the design is stunning.

## MATERIALS

**Approx total:** 1065 (1331, 1664, 2080, 2600, 3120, 3744, 4493)yd/969 (1211, 1514, 1893, 2366, 2839, 3407, 4089)m silk/wool blend worsted weight yarn

**Color A:** 369 (461, 576, 720, 900, 1080, 1296, 1555)yd/337 (422, 527, 658, 823, 988, 1185, 1422)m in variegated grays and blues

**Color B:** 266 (333, 416, 520, 650, 780, 936, 1123)yd/243 (304, 380, 475, 594, 713, 856, 1027)m in variegated browns

**Color C:** 348 (435, 544, 680, 850, 1020, 1224, 1469)yd/318 (398, 497, 622, 777, 933, 1119, 1343)m in variegated silver and gray

**Knitting needles**

4.5mm (Size 7 U.S.) circular needle 36"/91.5cm long *or size to obtain gauge*

4mm (Size 6 U.S.) circular needle 36"/91.5cm long

4.5mm (Size 7 U.S.) circular needle 16"/40cm long and double-pointed needles

4mm (Size 6 U.S.) double-pointed needles

Stitch holder

4 stitch markers
(1 in a contrasting color)

Darning needle for weaving in ends

## GAUGE

5 sts and 7 rows = 1" in St st using 4.5mm (Size 7 U.S.) needles

*Always take time to check your gauge.*

# Instructions

Body and sleeves are knit in the round to the armholes. Pieces are joined at the yoke and worked in one piece to the neck.

## Body

With A and larger 36" circular needle, cast on 192 (208, 240, 256, 272, 288, 320, 336) sts. Work in Garter Stitch for 6 rows. Join, placing a marker to note start of round.

**BEG COLORWORK**

With A and B, work Chart A patt around all sts until piece measures 4 (4, 4.25, 4.25, 4.5, 4.75, 5, 5.25)"/10 (10, 11, 11, 11.5, 12, 12.5, 13.5)cm from start of A/B section edge. Break B.

With C, work 4 rounds of Garter St.

With A, work 4 rounds of Garter St.

Cont with A and C, work Chart A patt around all sts until piece measures 8 (8.25, 8.5, 9, 9.75, 10.5, 11.25, 11.25)"/20.5 (21, 21.5, 23, 25, 26.5, 28.5, 28.5)cm from start of A/C section.

With A, work 4 rounds of Garter St.

With C, work 2 rounds of Garter St.

Break A.

## SHAPE ARMHOLES

Divide work equally into front and back, and place on holder or separate piece of yarn—96 (104, 120, 128, 136, 144, 160, 168) sts each side.

Work back and forth on each piece as follows: BO 4 sts at start of next 2 rows and knit rem sts—88 (96, 112, 120, 128, 136, 152, 160) sts rem. Break C. Slip sts onto holder or separate piece of yarn to work later.

## Sleeves (make 2)

With A and larger double-pointed needles, cast on 34 (34, 48, 48, 50, 52, 52, 54) sts. Join to knit in the round, placing marker to indicate start of round.

Work in k2, p2 ribbing for 2"/5cm, then with smaller double-pointed needles and C work 2"/5cm more of ribbing.

Switch back to larger double-pointed needles and with C work 4 rounds of Garter St. With A and C, work charted pattern across all sts and AT THE SAME TIME inc 1 st each at beg and end of round every 4 (2, 4, 4, 4, 2, 2, 2) rounds 23 (26, 21, 24, 25, 27, 29, 31) times—80 (86, 90, 96, 100, 106, 110, 116) sts. Change to 16" circular needle when the stitches no longer fit on the dpns. If necessary, work even until sleeve measures 17.5 (18, 18.5, 19, 19.5, 20, 20.5, 21)"/44.5 (45.5, 47, 48.5, 49.5, 51, 52, 53.5)cm from cast-on row.

With A, work 4 rounds of Garter St.

With C, work 2 rounds of Garter St.

Break A.

## SHAPE ARMHOLES

Work back and forth as follows: BO 4 sts at start of next 2 rows and knit rem sts—72 (78, 82, 88, 92, 98, 102, 108) sts rem. Break C. Slip sts onto holder or separate piece of yarn to work later.

## Yoke

Slip all sts onto larger 36" circular needle, placing marker between each section—72 (78, 82, 88, 92, 98, 102, 108) sts left sleeve, 88 (96, 112, 120, 128, 136, 152, 160) sts front, 72 (78, 82, 88, 92, 98, 102, 108) sts right sleeve, 88 (96, 112, 120, 128, 136, 152, 160) sts back—320 (348, 388, 416, 440, 468, 508, 536) sts total.

**Note:** Use a contrasting marker where left sleeve meets front to note start of round.

Starting at contrasting marker, with A work 4 rounds of Garter St.

**Next round:** With A and B, start Chart A patt around all sts.

Following charted colorwork pattern as est around entire yoke, and always working 1 st on either side of each marker as a knit st, work raglan dec as follows:

**Rounds 1 and 2:** (Work to 3 sts before next marker, k2tog-LS, k1, sm, k1, k2tog-RS) rep for each marker.

**Round 3:** Work all sts with no decreasing—16 sts decreased over last 3 rounds.

Rep last 3 rounds while working in colorwork as est until 72 (76, 84, 80, 80, 92, 92, 88) sts rem. Change to larger 16" circular needle when stitches no longer fit on longer needle. Turn work.

Neck opening should measure approx 14.5 (15, 17, 16, 16, 18.5, 18.5, 18)"/37 (38, 39.5, 40.5, 42, 43, 44.5, 45.5)cm in circumference.

**NECK SHAPING**
Work back and forth with short row shaping as follows:

**Next row (WS):** Working back over left sleeve, back, and right sleeve, cont in colorwork as est with no decreasing. Stop at marker between right sleeve and front, W&T.

**Next row (RS):** Cont in patt as est, work back to point where left sleeve meets back, W&T.

**Next row (WS):** Cont in patt as est, work to point where right sleeve meets back, W&T.

Return to working in the round, and with A, work 6 rounds of Garter St.

Switch to smaller 16" circular needle, and with C work k2, p2 ribbing for 8 rounds or work desired collar length. BO all sts loosely in ribbing.

# Finishing
Block pieces. Sew small seam at hem. Sew sleeve and under-arm seams. Weave in ends.

## This sweater was knit with:
Alchemy's *Synchronicity*, 50% silk, 50% merino wool, 118yd/107m, 1.75oz/50g per skein
(A) 8 balls, color 60C San Fran Sky
(B) 6 balls, color 55C Montrant Path
(C) 8 balls, color 26M Platinum

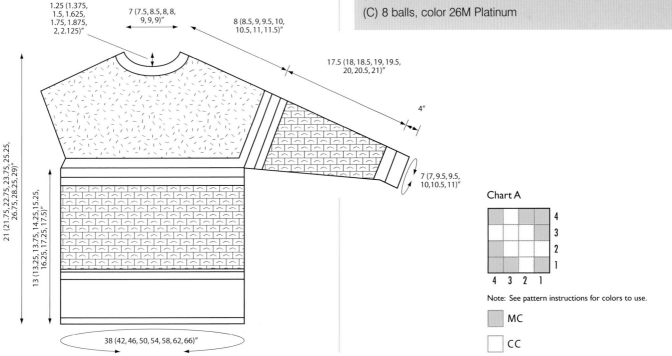

1.25 (1.375, 1.5, 1.625, 1.75, 1.875, 2, 2.125)"

7 (7.5, 8.5, 8, 8, 9, 9, 9)"

8 (8.5, 9, 9.5, 10, 10.5, 11, 11.5)"

17.5 (18, 18.5, 19, 19.5, 20, 20.5, 21)"

4"

7 (7, 9.5, 9.5, 10, 10.5, 11)"

21 (21.75, 22.75, 23.75, 25.25, 26.75, 28.25, 29)"

13 (13.25, 13.75, 14.25, 15.25, 16.25, 17.25, 17.5)"

38 (42, 46, 50, 54, 58, 62, 66)"

**Chart A**

| | | 4 |
| | | 3 |
| | | 2 |
| | | 1 |
| 4 | 3 | 2 | 1 |

Note: See pattern instructions for colors to use.

▨ MC

☐ CC

**SKILL LEVEL**
Easy

**FINISHED
MEASUREMENTS**
20 x 14"/51 by 35.5 cm

# Variegated Dog Kerchief

Your dog will be the fashion plate of the neighborhood with this stylish neckerchief. It's worked in one piece, even though it looks like the contrasting border was made separately.

**MATERIALS**
**Approx total:** 100yd/91m silk/wool blend worsted weight yarn

**Color A:** 80yd/73m in variegated grays and blues

**Color B:** 20yd/18m in variegated browns

**Knitting needles**
4.5mm (Size 7 U.S.)
*or size to obtain gauge*

Darning needle for weaving in ends

**GAUGE**
5 sts and 7 rows =
1"/2.5cm in Garter Stitch

*Always take time to check your gauge.*

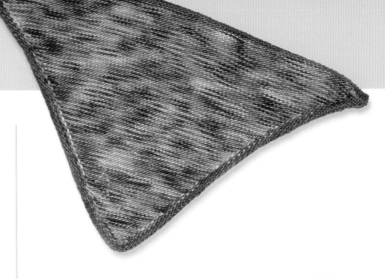

# Instructions

The kerchief is shaped with short rows (see page 15) to form a triangle.

## Kerchief

With a strand of B, cast on 101 sts and work in Garter Stitch for 4 rows.

**Row 1 (RS):** Slip 4 sts, with A knit to last 4 sts, W&T.

**Row 2 (WS):** Slip 4 sts, purl to the last 4 sts, W&T.

**Row 3:** Knit to 1 st before wrapped st from previous row, W&T.

**Row 4:** Purl to 1 st before wrapped st from previous row, W&T.

**Repeat rows 3 and 4,** working 1 st less in each row until 1 st remains in short row section.

**Next row (RS):** Knit to last A stitch, being careful to lift the wrap from each stitch up onto the left-hand needle and knit it along with the stitch. W&T next st (first st in B, 4th st in from edge of work).

**Next row (WS):** Purl to center st, pm, purl center st, pm, purl to last A st in row, lifting the wraps from each st up onto the left-hand needle and purling it along with the stitch. Break yarn, leaving a 6"/15cm tail. W&T next st (first st in B, 4th st in from edge of work).

**Next row (RS):** With B, k to marker, YO, sm, k1, sm, YO, k to last wrapped st (first B st). Lift wraps up onto left-hand needle and knit them together with stitch. W&T.

**Next row (WS):** K to marker, YO, sm, k1, sm, YO, k to last wrapped st, lift wrap up onto left-hand needle and knit together with stitch, W&T.

**Rep last 2 rows** until all 4 B edge sts have been worked and 4 rows of garter have been completed, inc 2 sts at center of work in each row. Bind off all 109 sts very loosely.

Steam block, weave in ends.

### This kerchief was knit with:

Alchemy's Synchronicity, 50% silk, 50% merino wool, 118yd/107m, 1.75oz/50g per skein
(A) 1 skein, color 60C San Fran Sky
(B) 1 skein, color 55C Montreat Path

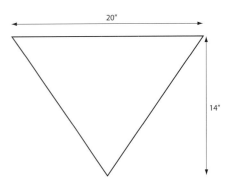

**SKILL LEVEL**
Easy

**FINISHED MEASUREMENTS**
**Foot Length:** 7.5 (8.5, 9.5, 10.5, 11.5)"/19 (21.5, 24, 26.5, 29)cm
**Foot Circumference:** 7 (7.75, 8.5, 9.25, 10)"/18 (19.5, 21.5, 23.5, 25.5)cm

**MATERIALS**
**Approx total:** 162 (171, 188, 205, 222)yd/147 (156, 171, 187, 202)m washable chunky wool yarn in variegated neutrals

**Knitting needles**
3.75mm (Size 5 U.S.)
2 circular needles 16"/41cm long *or size to obtain gauge*

3.5mm (Size 4 U.S.)
2 circular needles 16"/41cm long for leg (optional)

Darning needle for weaving in ends

**GAUGE**
6 sts and 7 rows = 1"/2.5cm in St st

*Always take time to check your gauge.*

# Easy Toe-Up Socks

The hardest part of making these socks is getting the stitches cast on. After that, they zip by on two circular needles, and there's no finishing except for weaving in the ends.

# Instructions

Sock is worked from the toe up on two circular needles (see page 17). The heel is shaped with short rows (see page 15).

## Sock Toe

Holding 2 circs parallel in your right hand, cast on 12 sts by casting on 1 stitch on one needle, then casting on 1 st on the other needle six times. Work back and forth, holding the circs close together, until all sts are cast on.

**Round 1:** Always working the sts on circ #1 with the opposite end of circ #1, k1, k into the back, then into the front of the next st, k to the last 2 sts on circ #1, k into the back and front of the next st, k the last st. Move to circ #2, and repeat.

**Round 2:** Always working the sts with the opposite end of the same needle on which they sit, knit all sts.

**Repeat the last 2 rounds** until there are 44 (48, 52, 56, 60) sts, then repeat only round 2, working even with no shaping until the sock is long enough so that when fit on foot it reaches the ankle bone, (approx 5.25 (6, 6.75, 7.25, 8)"/13.5 (15, 17,18.5, 20.5)cm, or desired length to heel.

## Short Row Heel Part 1

Worked back and forth in short rows, only on circ #1.

**Row 1 (RS):** K to last st, W&T.

**Row 2 (WS):** P to last st, W&T.

**Row 3:** Cont in St st, work to 1 st before last wrapped st, W&T.

**Rep row 3** until 6 (6, 6, 8, 8) sts rem unwrapped in center of circ #1. End with a RS row.

**Next row (WS):** P to end of circ #1, slipping the wrap from each st up onto the left-hand needle and working it, along with the st it was wrapped around, together as a purl st.

**Next round (RS):** K to end of circ #1, slipping the wrap and working it in the same manner as in previous row, this time knitting all sts, then continue around sts on circ #2.

## Short Row Heel Part 2

Worked back and forth in short rows, only on circ #1.

**Row 1 (RS):** On circ #1, work 14 (15, 16, 18, 19) sts, W&T.

**Row 2 (WS):** P3 (3, 3, 4, 4) sts, W&T.

**Row 3:** Cont in St st, work to 1 st past last wrapped st, working wrap along with stitch as previously done, W&T.

**Rep row 3** until all sts have been worked. End with a WS row.

**Next round:** Return to knitting in the round. Working the sts with the opposite end of the same needle on which they sit, knit all sts.

## Ribbed Leg

**Next round:** (K2, p2) rep across circ #1 and continue across circ #2, moving down a needle size if a tighter leg is desired. Continue working K2, p2 ribbing in the round on 2 circs as est until leg is desired length.

### ELASTIC BIND OFF

**Preparation round:** (K1, sl 1, p1, sl 1) rep to end of round.

**Bind-off round:** (K2tog-tbl, slip st created back onto LH needle, [p2tog, slip st created back onto LH needle] twice, k2tog-tbl, slip st created back onto LH needle) rep to end of round, working VERY loosely. Cut yarn, leaving an 8"/20.5cm tail, and pull through.

If desired, with a strand of yarn and darning needle, tighten up sts on either side of short row heel.

Weave in ends.

**These socks were knit with:**

1 skein of Artyarns; *Handpaint Stripe Superwash*, 100% merino wool, 188yd/171m, 3 1/2oz/100g per skein, color HS140

SKILL LEVEL
Easy

FINISHED
MEASUREMENTS
**Foot Length:** 3 (3.25, 3.5, 4,
4.5)"/7.5 (8.5, 9, 10, 11.5)cm
**Foot Circumference:**
4.5 (5, 5.5, 6, 6.5)"/11.5
(12.5,14,15, 16.5)cm

MATERIALS
**Approx total:** 48 (60, 72, 84,
96)yd/44 (55, 66, 77, 88)m
washable chunky wool yarn
in variegated neutrals

**Knitting needles**
3.75mm (Size 5 U.S.)
double-pointed needles
*or size to obtain gauge*

3.5mm (Size 4 U.S.)
double-pointed needles

Darning needle for
weaving in ends

GAUGE
6 sts and 7 rows = 1" in
St st using 3.75mm (Size
5 U.S.) needles

*Always take time to check
your gauge.*

# Superwash Mutt-Luks

If you go hiking in snowy weather or if you plan to enter the Iditarod,
your dog will thank you for these comfy foot warmers. Machine-washable
yarn was chosen for these doggie slippers for obvious reasons. Because
there's little foot shaping, these socks are very easy to make.

## Instructions

These mutt-luks are worked in the round on double-pointed needles from the cuff down.

## Cuff

With smaller needles, cast on 24 (28, 28, 32, 36) sts. Join to work in the round.

Work in k2, p2 ribbing for 2.75 (3,3.25,3.5, 3.75)"/7 (7.5, 8.5, 9, 9.5)cm.

## Foot

Change to larger needles and St st and inc 3 (2, 5, 4, 3) sts evenly around—27 (30, 33, 36, 39) sts. Work even with no increasing for 8 (9, 9, 10, 12) rows.

## Toe

**Next round:** (K 7 [8, 9, 10, 11] sts, k2tog, pm), rep around.

**Next round:** (K to 2 sts before marker, k2tog, sm) rep around.

Rep last round until 3 sts rem. Cut yarn, leaving an 8"/20.3cm tail. Pull tail through rem 3 sts and draw closed. Weave in ends.

## Finishing

Stretch finished mutt-luk over a circle approx 2.75 (3,3.25,3.5, 4)"/7 (7.5, 8.5, 9, 10)cm diameter. A jar lid works well. Using a machine-washable, flexible fabric paint like Jones Tones Stretchy Fabric Paint, paint a paw print on one side of the mutt-luk to aid in traction. Allow to dry thoroughly, following manufacturer's instructions for setting paint if necessary.

**Note:** When using fabric paint or some texturing agent for the bottom of slippers or socks, pull the fabric taught over a frame (I used a spaghetti sauce lid for these mutt-luks) and paint the fabric as it's stretched. Allow it to dry completely before removing the frame.

These mutt-luks were knit with:

1 (1, 2, 2, 2) skein of Artyarns; *Handpaint Stripe Superwash*, 100% merino wool, 188yd/171m, 3½oz/100g per skein, color HS140

# Men's Knit Zip Front Pullover

With texture on the body and stripes on the sleeves, this sweater
will not be boring to knit. It features a unique double-knit edging
to frame the zipper placket, so sewing in the zipper is a cinch.

## MATERIALS

**Approx total** 1280 (1360,
1440, 1520, 1600, 1760, 1920,
2080)yd/1165 (1238, 1310,
1383, 1456, 1602, 1747,
1893)m 100% alpaca light
worsted weight yarn

**Color A:** 240 (255, 270, 285,
300, 330, 360, 390)yd/218
(232, 246, 259, 273, 300, 328,
355)m in light tan

**Color B:** 240 (255, 270, 285,
300, 330, 360, 390)yd/218
(232, 246, 259, 273, 300, 328,
355)m in brown

**Color C:** 800 (850, 900, 950,
1000, 1100, 1200, 1300)yd/728
(774, 819, 865, 910, 1001,
1092, 1183)m in copper

**Knitting needles**
4mm (Size 6 U.S.)
*or size to obtain gauge*

3.75mm (Size 5 U.S.)

7 to 10"/18 to 25.5cm zipper
(depending on size of sweater)

Sewing needle and
thread to match B

2 stitch holders

Darning needle to
weave in ends

## GAUGE

5.25 sts and 7 rows = 1"/2.5cm
in Chart A Cable Patt using
4mm (Size 6 U.S.) needles

5 sts and 7 rows = 1"/2.5cm
in Chart B Patt using 4mm
(Size 6 U.S.) needles

*Always take time to check
your gauge.*

## Special Pattern Stitches & Techniques

### I-CORD BIND OFF

Cast on 2 sts at start of row using Cable Cast On. (K2,
k2togLS. Slip 3 sts from RH needle back onto LH needle. Pull
yarn taut across back of work.) Repeat across work until 3 sts
rem, k3tog-LS.

### DOUBLE-KNIT SLIPPED ST (DKSS) EDGE

**Row 1 (RS):** K1, wyif sl1,
k1, work to last 3 sts, k1,
wyif sl1, k1.

**Row 2 (WS):** Wyif sl1, k1,
wyif sl1, work to last 3 sts,
wyif sl1, k1, wyif sl1.

**Note:** on RS rows wyif means yarn to the RS of work. On WS
rows wyif means yarn to the WS of work.

Rep rows 1 and 2 for patt.

# Instructions

This sweater is knit flat in pieces. The body is made with a
solid color in a cable pattern. The sleeves are worked in stripes.

## Back

With a single strand of A and larger needle, CO 84 (90, 96,
102, 108, 114, 126, 138) sts. Work 6 rows of Garter St, end
with a WS row.

**Next row (RS):** Beg with st 1 of row 1, work Chart B Cable
Patt across all sts. Cont in charted patt as est until piece
measures 14.75 (15, 15.25, 15.5, 15.5, 16, 17, 18.25)"/37.5
(38.5, 38, 39.5, 39.5, 40.5, 43, 46.5)cm from cast-on edge.
End with a WS row.

## ARMHOLE SHAPING

**Next row (RS):** BO 4 (4, 4, 4, 4, 6, 6, 6) sts at start of each armhole edge, then BO 2 (2, 3, 3, 3, 3, 3, 3) sts at armhole edge twice—68 (74, 76, 82, 88, 90, 102, 114) sts rem. Cont in charted patt, work even until armhole depth measures 8 (8.5, 8.5, 9, 9, 9.5, 10, 10.5)"/20.5 (21.5, 21.5, 23, 23, 24, 25.5, 26.5)cm. End with a WS row.

## SHOULDER SHAPING

**Next row (RS):** BO 8 (9, 10, 9, 10, 10, 12, 13) sts from start of next 6 rows. Slip rem 20 (20, 16, 28, 28, 30, 30 36) neck sts to stitch holder.

# Front

Work as for back to just past armhole shaping. End with a WS row.

**Next row (RS):** Work across 34 (37, 40, 41, 44, 45, 51, 57) sts. Join a 2nd ball of yarn and work to end. Working both sides at the same time and cont in patt as est, work fronts as follows:

**Next row (WS):** With A, work to 4 sts before center divide, pm, with a strand of B (k1, wyif sl1) twice. Cont with left front edge and a new strand of B, (wyif sl1, k1) twice, pm, with A work in patt as est to end of row.

**Next row (RS):** With A, work to marker, sm, with B p1, k1, wyif sl1, k1. Cont with right front edge, with B k1, wyif sl1, k1, p1, sm, with A work in patt as est to end of row. Be sure to twist yarns between colors to prevent a hole. Rep last 2 rows, cont in patt as est, until piece measures same as back to shoulder shaping. Shape shoulders as for back, slip rem sts to holder.

# Sleeves (make 2)

With B and a larger needle, cast on 38 (40, 40, 42, 42, 42, 44, 46) sts. Work 6 rows of Garter St, end with a WS row.

**Sizes 32 to 44:** Inc 1 st each edge every alternate 2nd and 4th rows 21 (23, 23, 24, 24, 27) times.

**Sizes 48 and 52 only:** Inc 1 st each edge every other row 28 (30) times.

Sleeve has 80 (86, 86, 90, 90, 96, 100, 106) sts after final inc row worked.

AT SAME TIME starting with a RS row, work 24 row Chart A Stripe Patt as follows:

With B, work 2 rows of Garter St.

With A, work 4 rows of St st.

With C, work 2 rows of Garter St.

With C, work 4 rows of St st.

With C, work 2 rows of Garter St.

With A, work 4 rows of St st.

With B, work 2 rows of Garter St.

With B, work 4 rows of St st.

Repeat stripe pattern until sleeve measures 16.25 (16.5, 16.25, 17, 16.75, 16.75, 17.25, 17.5)"/41.5 (42, 41.5, 43, 42.5, 42.5, 44, 44.5)cm from cast-on edge.

## CAP SHAPING

BO 6 (6, 6, 6, 6, 7, 7, 7) sts at start of next 2 rows, then BO 4 (4, 4, 4, 3, 3, 3, 3) sts at start of next 4 rows, then [BO 3 (3, 2, 3, 3, 2, 2, 2) sts at start of next 2 rows, work 2 rows even] twice, work 6 rows even, then BO 2 (2, 2, 2, 2, 2, 2, 2) sts at start of next 2 rows. BO rem 44 (50, 52, 54, 58, 64, 68, 74) sts.

# Finishing

Block pieces. Sew shoulder seams. Sew underarm and side seams. Sew in sleeves.

## COLLAR

With B and a smaller needle, slip right neck edge sts from holder to needle, slip back sts to needle, and end by slipping rem left neck edge sts to needle.

Cont to work edge sts in DKSS edging as est, work rem sts in Garter St until collar measures 4"/10cm or desired length.

Work I-Cord bind off as follows: K3, slip 3 sts back to the left-hand needle, (k2, k2tog-RS, slip 3 sts back to the left-hand needle) rep across all sts until 6 sts rem total (including 3 I-cord sts).

**Next row (RS):** Sl3 sts back to the left-hand needle, k2, k2tog-LS.

**Next row (RS):** Sl3 sts back to the left-hand needle, k1, VDD.

**Next row (RS):** Sl2 sts back to the left-hand needle, VDD, break yarn leaving an 8"/20.5cm tail, pull tail through last loop.

Weave in ends.

**Chart A**
**Stripe Patt**

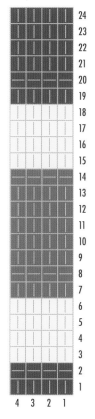

24
23
22
21
20
19
18
17
16
15
14
13
12
11
10
9
8
7
6
5
4
3
2
1

4 3 2 1

☐ A - Light Tan
■ B - Brown
▦ C - Copper

**Chart B**
**Cable Patt**

6
5
4
3
2
1

6 5 4 3 2 1

 K on RS, P on WS

— P on RS, K on WS

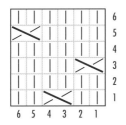 TW2R - Twist 2 sts to the right: K the 2nd st on LH needle, then without slipping st off needle, K the first st on LH needle. Slip both off needle together.

**ZIPPER**

Measure from top of collar to start of center front divide. Purchase a zipper 1/4 to 1/2"/.5 to 1.5cm shorter than this measurement. If you can't find a zipper the correct size, use a longer zipper and, with button thread, tack across the zipper at desired length.

Pin zipper into place along center front edges. Hand-stitch in place, working just behind DKSS edging to hide sewing sts. Trim bottom of zipper below tack. Some zipper packaging includes instructions for this; this technique works best with a nylon zipper. You can also use a shorter zipper and sew fronts closed up to point where zipper starts.

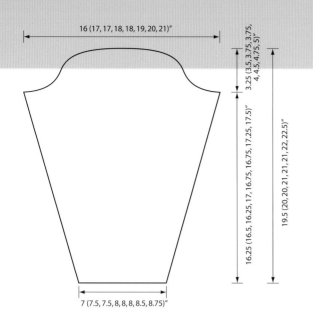

16 (17, 17, 18, 18, 19, 20, 21)"

3.25 (3.5, 3.75, 3.75, 4, 4.5, 4.75, 5)"

16.25 (16.5, 16.25, 17, 16.75, 16.75, 17.25, 17.5)"

19.5 (20, 20, 21, 21, 21, 22, 22.5)"

7 (7.5, 7.5, 8, 8, 8, 8.5, 8.75)"

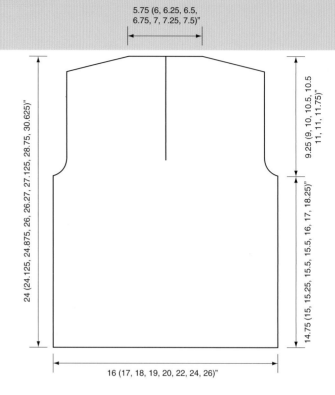

5.75 (6, 6.25, 6.5, 6.75, 7, 7.25, 7.5)"

9.25 (9, 10, 10.5, 10.5 11, 11, 11.75)"

24 (24.125, 24.875, 26, 26.27, 27.125, 28.75, 30.625)"

14.75 (15, 15.25, 15.5, 15.5, 16, 17, 18.25)"

16 (17, 18, 19, 20, 22, 24, 26)"

## This sweater was knit with:

Blue Sky Alpacas' *Sport Weight*, 100% Alpaca,
110yd/100m, 1.75oz/50g per skein
(A) 2 (2, 2, 3, 3, 3, 3, 4)  skeins, color 004 Natural Lt Tan
(B) 2 (2, 2, 3, 3, 3, 3, 4)  skeins, color 008 Natural Strky Brown
(C) 7 (8, 8, 9, 9, 3, 3, 12)  skeins, color 002 Natural Copper

## Scott Simpson
Sacramento, California

"Knitting has changed me in that I
now complete things that I have started.
I've become much more calm and
patient in my everyday life."

**SKILL LEVEL**
Intermediate

**FINISHED MEASUREMENTS**
**Chest:** 42 (44, 48, 50, 54, 58)"/106.5 (111.75, 122, 127, 137, 147.25)cm
*See Men's Sizes on page 20 for tips on choosing the correct size.*

**MATERIALS**
**Approx total:** 1504 (1880, 2350, 2820, 3384, 4061)yd/1369, 1711, 2139, 2566, 3079, 3696)m wool DK weight yarn

**Color A:** 640 (800, 1000, 1200, 1440, 1728 )yd/582 (728, 910, 1092, 1310, 1572)m in tan

**Color B:** 448 (560, 700, 840, 1008, 1210 )yd/408 (510, 637, 764, 917, 1101)m in black

**Color C:** 416 (520, 650, 780, 936, 1123 )yd/379 (473, 592, 710, 852, 1022)m in ecru

**Knitting needles**
3.75mm (Size 5 U.S.) circular knitting needle 29"/73.5cm long, 12"/30.5cm long, and double-pointed needles *or size to obtain gauge*

3.5mm (Size 4 U.S.) circular knitting needle 29"/73.5cm long, 12"/30.5cm long, and double-pointed needles

Darning needle for sewing seams

**GAUGE**
6 sts and 7 rows = 1"/2.5cm in Stockinette Stitch using 3.75mm (Size 5 U.S.) needles

*Always take time to check your gauge.*

# Shades of Gray Sweater

Knitted in DK weight wool yarn, this sweater is lightweight, even though it's worked with multiple colors. The neutral colors are worked in bold geometric pattern, giving the sweater a contemporary and fun feel.

# Instructions

The body and sleeves are worked in the round to the armholes, at which point pieces are worked back and forth.

## Body

With smaller circular needle and B, cast on 252 (260, 292, 300, 320, 352) sts. Join to knit in the round.

**Note:** If desired, work a few rows of k2, p2 ribbing before joining to prevent work from becoming twisted on the needle.

Work in k2, p2 ribbing until piece measures 3"/7.5cm.

**Next round:** Dec 2 (0, 2, 0, 0, 2) sts evenly around—250 (260, 290, 300, 320, 350) sts.

### START COLORWORK

**Next round:** Place a marker to note start of round. Change to larger circular needle and beg with st 1, row 1 of Chart A, rep 10 st patt around all sts, being careful not to pull floats too tight behind work.

**Work colorwork rounds as follows:** Work 26 rows of Chart A, then work 26 rows of Chart B, 3 (4, 4, 4, 5, 5) times, then work first 10 (0, 0, 10, 0, 10) rows of Chart B, and work an additional 2 (0, 0, 2, 0, 2) rows in Color C. End by working all 26 rows of Chart A.

AT THE SAME TIME, when body measures 11.25 (12.75, 12.25, 13.5, 15, 16.25)"/28.5 (32.5, 31, 34.5, 38, 41.5)cm from end of ribbing, divide sts equally for front and back—125 (130, 145, 150, 160, 175) sts each side.

### UPPER BACK

Working back and forth from this point on, shape armhole as follows: BO 6 (6, 8, 8, 8, 8) sts at beg of next 2 rows, then BO 4 sts at beg of next 2 rows—97 (102, 113, 118, 128, 143) sts rem.

Work even in patt as est until armhole measures 8 (8.5, 9, 9.5, 10, 10.5)"/20.5 (21.5, 23, 24, 25.5, 26.5)cm.

Shape shoulders as follows: BO 8 (8, 10, 10, 12, 14)sts at start of next 4 rows, then BO 7 (9, 10, 11, 12, 15) sts at start of next 2 rows. BO rem 51 (52, 53, 56, 56, 57) sts.

### UPPER FRONT

Work as for Upper Back until front measures 6.25 (7, 7, 7.375, 7.75, 8.125)"/16 (2.6, 18, 18.5, 19.5, 20.5)cm from start of armhole shaping.

### NECK SHAPING

Work across 43 (45, 50, 54, 57, 64) sts, join 2nd ball of yarn and BO center 12 (12, 12, 14, 14, 14) sts and work across row—37 (39, 44, 47, 50, 57) sts rem on each shoulder.

Working both shoulders at the same time with separate balls of yarn, BO 5 (5, 4, 4, 4, 4) at each neck edge every row 2 times, then BO 1 (1, 1, 2, 1, 1) at each neck edge every other row 2 times, then BO 1 (1, 2, 2, 2, 2) at each neck edge every 4th row 2 times—23 (25, 30, 31, 36, 43) sts rem on each shoulder.

AT THE SAME TIME when armhole depth measures 8 (8.5, 9, 9.5, 10, 10.5)"/20.5 (21.5, 23, 24, 25.5, 26.5)cm, BO shoulders as for Upper Back.

## Sleeves (make 2)

With smaller double-pointed needles and B, cast on 52 (52, 56, 56, 56, 60) sts. Work in k2, p2 ribbing as for body, working several rows before joining to reduce the risk of twisting the fabric, if desired. When ribbing measures 4"/10cm, dec 2 (dec 2, inc 4, inc 4, inc 4, inc 0) sts—50 (50, 60, 60, 60, 60) sts.

**Next round:** Place a marker to note start of round. Change to larger double-pointed needles and beg with st 1, row 1 of Chart A, rep 10 st patt around all sts, being careful not to pull floats too tight. Rep all 26 rows of Chart A and AT THE SAME TIME inc 1 st at center marker alternately every row and every other row (for example, inc 1 st first row, inc 1 st in second row, inc 0 sts in third row, repeat), staggering increases so they fall on either side of the center marker.

Change to 12" long circular needle when sts no longer fit on dpns.

Working new sts into colorwork patt as est, inc until there are 108 (114, 120, 126, 132, 138) sts in entire sleeve. Work even until sleeve measures 17 (17.5, 18, 18.5, 19, 19.5)"/43 (44.5, 45.5, 47, 48.5, 49.5)cm from end of ribbing.

**CAP SHAPING**

Remove marker. Working back and forth from this point on, shape sleeve cap as follows: BO 7 (7, 7, 9, 9, 9) sts at start of next 2 rows, then BO 4 (4, 4, 4, 6, 6) sts at start of next 4 rows, then [BO 3 (3, 4, 3, 3, 2) sts at start of next 2 rows, work 2 rows even] 3 times, then [BO 3 (3, 3, 3, 2, 3) sts at start of next 2 rows, work 6 rows even] 4 (4, 4, 5, 5, 5) times. BO rem 57 (63, 66, 68, 71, 75) sts.

# Finishing

Block all pieces. Weave in ends. Sew shoulder seams. Pin sleeves in place at armhole openings. Starting at center top and working down the back to center underarm, sew sleeve in place. Repeat for front of sleeve. Sew in 2nd sleeve in the same manner.

**NECKBAND**

With smaller 12"-long circular needle and B, pick up and knit 84 (88, 104, 108, 112, 116) sts around neck opening. Work in k2, p2 ribbing for 1.5"/3.4cm. Bind off very loosely with larger needles.

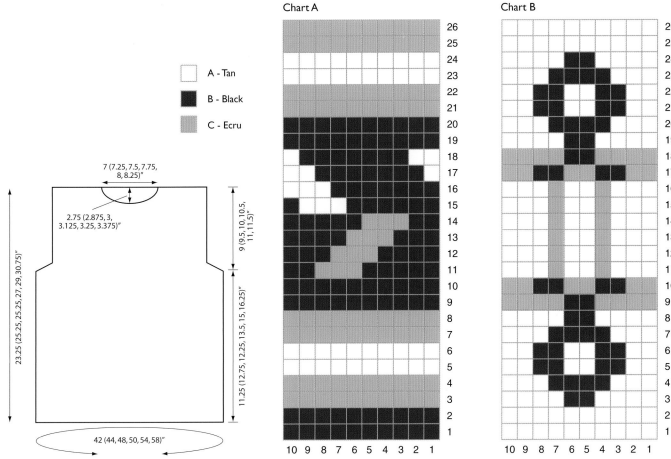

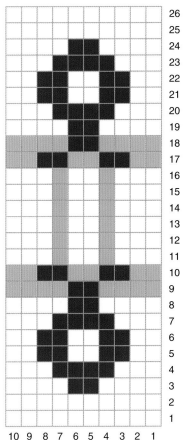

Chart A

Chart B

A - Tan

B - Black

C - Ecru

7 (7.25, 7.5, 7.75, 8, 8.25)"

2.75 (2.875, 3, 3.125, 3.25, 3.375)"

9 (9.5, 10, 10.5, 11, 11.5)"

23.25 (25.25, 25.25, 27, 29, 30.75)"

11.25 (12.75, 12.25, 13.5, 15, 16.25)"

42 (44, 48, 50, 54, 58)"

## This sweater was knit with:

Karabella's *Aurora* 4, 100% extra-fine merino, 197yds/180m, 1.75oz/50g per skein:

(A) 3 (4, 5, 6, 7, 8) skeins color 1, Tan
(B) 2 (2, 3, 4, 5, 6) skeins color 1148, Black
(C) 2 (2, 3, 3, 4, 5) skeins color 1359, Ecru

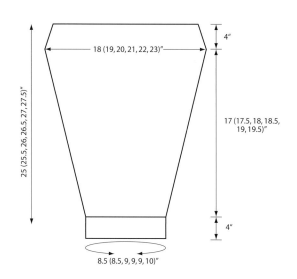

18 (19, 20, 21, 22, 23)"

4"

25 (25.5, 26, 26.5, 27, 27.5)"

17 (17.5, 18, 18.5, 19, 19.5)"

4"

8.5 (8.5, 9, 9, 9, 10)"

MEN WHO KNIT

### Jon Thumin
Denver, Colorado

"Now that I knit, I can express myself in a thousand different ways, and have something wonderful to show for it. I like working with natural fibers like wool and silk; they are a connection to the environment."

# Boy Toy

What could be more fun to knit than a chew toy for your favorite canine friend? This boy toy is made with the leftover yarn from the Shades of Gray Sweater on page 47, but you can easily substitute the yarn left over from any knitting project.

## Special Stitch
**I-BOBBLE**

K3 sts into next st.

(Slip these 3 sts back to the left-hand needle and knit) 4 times.

# Instructions

This chew toy is worked in the round on double-pointed needles. Ends are woven in and pieces are stuffed as you go.

## Shoes

With smaller dpns and A, cast on 12 sts. Divide sts evenly between 3 dpns and join to work in the round.

Work in St st for 8 rounds.

**SHAPE TOE**

Worked back and forth in short rows as follows:

**Row 1 (RS):** K8, W&T.

**Row 2 (WS):** P7, W&T.

**Row 3:** K6, W&T.

**Row 4:** P5, W&T.

**Row 5:** K4, W&T.

**Row 6:** P3, W&T.

**Row 7:** K2, W&T.

**Row 8:** P3, W&T.

**Row 9:** K4, W&T.

**Row 10:** P5, W&T.

**Row 11:** K6, W&T.

**Row 12:** P7, W&T.

Begin working in rounds again, work in St st for 4 rounds.

Divide sts equally into front and back sts, place on holder.

Repeat for 2nd shoe.

## Pants

Slip all sts from both shoes onto larger dpns, keeping back shoe and front shoe sts placed so that both shoes point in the same direction—24 sts.

Weave in the ends at the toes of the shoes, closing them off at the same time.

With B begin working in St st in the round. Inc 1 st at each outer edge (outseam of the pants side) in each of the next 2 rows—28 sts.

Cont working in St st for 33 rounds.

## Hands

Work 1 round, making an I-Bobble on each outer edge.

## Sweater

Cont in St st and work stripe patt as follows:

(With A, work 2 rounds. With C, work 1 round) twice.

With A, work 2 rounds.

With B, work 3 rounds

With C, work 3 rounds

With B, work 3 rounds.

With A, work 4 rounds.

With A, inc 1 st at each outer (shoulder) edge—30 sts.

Work 4 rounds even, then inc 1 st at each outer edge in each of the next 2 rows—34 sts.

Work 2 rounds even.

Turn doll inside out. Weave in ends. Turn doll right side out again and fill the pants and sweater with fiberfill. Do not overfill, but make sure that filling is well distributed.

## Shoulders

Place 16 center front sts on one needle, and 9 sts on each of two other dpns, with the join at the center back. Work to shoulder edge, break yarn, leaving a 20"/51cm tail.

Join the outer 4 sts from the front and the back together with the 3-needle bind off to create a shoulder—5 sts rem on back needle just worked, 12 sts on front needle.

Continuing with tail, work across to other shoulder and repeat joining—5 sts rem on back needle just worked, 5 sts rem on previous back needle, 8 sts left on front needle, 18 sts total.

Work 1 round even.

## Head

Change to C and work in St st for 8 rounds.

**Next round:** Starting at center back, k2tog, k1, k2tog; next needle, k2tog, k4, k2tog; next needle, k2tog, k1, k2tog—12 sts rem.

Fill head with fiberfill.

**Next round:** VDD, k2tog, k2, k2tog, VDD. Break yarn, leaving a 9"/23cm tail. Draw tail through rem sts and pull tightly. Make a small knot at top of head and weave yarn into head.

## Finishing

With B and darning needle, stitch a "seam" up the center of the legs, ending about 6 rows before start of sweater. In the same manner, create two "seams" from the bobble-hands up to the shoulders, stopping about 8 rows from the top of the shoulder.

With C, embroider over each bobble-hand until it is completely covered, adding fingers if desired. Create 3 dimples on the front of the face by creating a tack where the eyes and nose would be.

### HAIR

With crochet hook, pull 3"/7.5cm pieces of A through the stitches at the top of the head starting at the center and work-ing out to the hairline until top of head is covered—do not overload the top of the head with hair! Using sharp scissors, trim hair into whatever hairstyle you desire.

## This toy was knit with:

Karabella's *Aurora* 4, 197yd/179m, 1.75oz/50g per skein:

(A) 1 skein, color 1148 Black

(B) 1 skein, color 1359 Ecru

(C) 1 skein, color 1 Tan

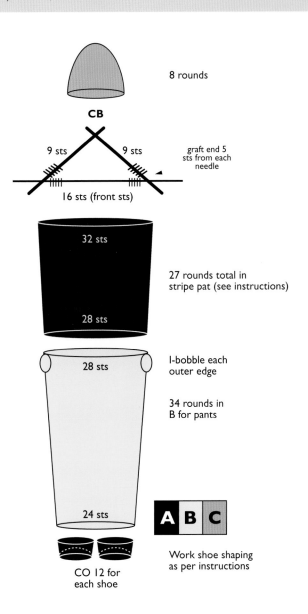

8 rounds

CB

9 sts · 9 sts

graft end 5 sts from each needle

16 sts (front sts)

32 sts

27 rounds total in stripe pat (see instructions)

28 sts

28 sts

I-bobble each outer edge

34 rounds in B for pants

24 sts

A B C

Work shoe shaping as per instructions

CO 12 for each shoe

53

## SKILL LEVEL
Easy

## FINISHED MEASUREMENTS
**Chest:** 36 (38, 40, 42, 44, 48, 52, 56)"/91.5 (96.5, 101.5, 106.5, 112, 122, 132, 142)cm
*See Men's Sizes on page 20 for tips on choosing the correct size.*

# Garter Ridge Stripe Pullover

The design is your classic men's pullover, but with a fashion twist. The easy stripe pattern keeps the knitting from getting boring and lends the sweater a pop of contemporary color.

## MATERIALS
**Approx total:** 1228 (1536, 1920, 2400, 2880, 3456, 4148, 4979)yd/1117 (1398, 1747, 2184, 2621, 3145, 3775, 4531)m of alpaca/silk/wool blend worsted weight yarn

**Color A:** 358 (448, 560, 700, 840, 1008, 1210, 1452)yd/326 (408, 510, 637, 764, 917, 1101, 1321)m in light green

**Color B:** 512 (640, 800, 1000, 1200, 1440, 1728, 2074)yd/466 (582, 728, 910, 1092, 1310, 1572, 1887)m in dark green

**Color C:** 358 (448, 560, 700, 840, 1008, 1210, 1452)yd/326 (408, 510, 637, 764, 917, 1101, 1321)m in purple

### Knitting needles
5mm (Size 8 U.S.) circular needle 29"/74cm long *or size to obtain gauge*

4.5mm (Size 7 U.S.) circular needle 29"/74cm long and 16"/41cm long

Tapestry needle for weaving in ends

### GAUGE
4.5 sts and 6 rows = 1"/2.5cm in St st using 5mm (Size 8 U.S.) needles

*Always take time to check your gauge.*

## Instructions
Body is worked in the round to armholes, then worked back and forth to the shoulders. Sleeves are worked back and forth. Pieces are sewn together after the knitting is complete.

## Body
With B and smaller 29" long circular needle, cast on 164 (172, 180, 188, 200, 216, 236, 252) sts. Work in k2, p2 ribbing for 4 rows. Join work and cont working in ribbing as est with yarn C for 4 rounds. Change to yarn B and work 4 more rounds of ribbing.

Change to larger needle and with yarn C work 2 rounds of Garter Stitch (k 1 round, p 1 round).

With A work 2 rounds of St st (k 2 rounds). Break A and C.

Cont with B, work in St st until piece measures 7.5 (8.5, 8.25, 9, 9, 9.75, 11.25, 12.5)"/19 (21.5, 21, 23, 23, 25, 28.5, 32) from cast on, work 40 rounds Chart A Stripe Patt as follows:

With A, k 2 rounds.

With C, k 1 round, p 1 round.

With B, k 8 rounds.

With C, k 1 round, p 1 round.

With A, k 12 rounds.

With C, k 1 round, p 1 round.

With B, k 8 rounds.

With C, k 1 round, p 1 round.

With A, k 2 rounds.

Cont in B with no further striping and AT SAME TIME when piece measures 11.25 (11.75, 11.5, 12, 12, 12.5, 13.5, 14.75)"/28.5 (30, 29, 30.5, 30.5, 32, 34.5 37.5)cm from top of ribbing, divide sts for front and back—82 (86, 90, 94, 100, 108, 118, 126) sts each side.

## Upper Back
With B work back and forth in St st until back measures 20.25 (21.25, 21, 22, 22, 23, 24.5, 26.25)"/51.5 (54, 53.5, 56, 56, 58.5, 62, 66.5)cm from cast-on edge.

### SHOULDER SHAPING
BO 7 (8, 8, 9, 10, 11, 12, 13) sts from start of next 4 rows, then BO 10 (10, 12, 11, 12, 13, 16, 17) sts from start of next 2 rows. BO rem 34 (34, 34, 36, 36, 38, 38, 40) sts.

## Upper Front
With B, work across 41 (43, 45, 47, 50, 54, 59, 63) sts, join 2nd ball of yarn and work to end.

### NECK SHAPING
Working both sides at once, BO 1 st at neck edge every other row 17 (17, 17, 18, 18, 19, 19, 20) sts 2 times, AND AT SAME TIME, when front measures 20.25 (21.25, 21, 22, 22, 23, 24.5, 26.25)"/51.5 (54, 53.5, 56, 56, 58.5, 62, 66.5)cm from cast-on edge, work shoulder shaping as for back.

## Sleeves (make 2)
With B and smaller needles, cast on 30 (30, 30, 32, 32, 32, 34, 34) sts. Work in k2, p2 ribbing for 4 rows. With C, cont in ribbing for 12 rows. Change to B and work 4 more rows of ribbing.

Change to larger needle and C. K 2 rows.

Change to B. Inc 1 st at start of every row 42 (46, 46, 50, 50, 54, 56, 60) sts—72 (76, 76, 82, 82, 86, 90, 94) sts. AT THE SAME TIME, when sleeve meas 15 (15.75, 15.75, 17, 17, 17.75, 19, 19.5)"/38.5 (40.4, 40.4, 43.6, 43.6, 45.5, 48.7, 50)cm from start of sleeve, work 40 rows of color striping as for body, continuing to shape sleeve. Work even until piece meas 18 (18.5, 18.5, 19.25, 19.25, 20, 20.75, 21.25) " 46.2 (47.4, 47.4, 49.4, 49.4, 51.3, 53.2, 54.5) from start of sleeve. BO all sts.

## Finishing
Block pieces, sew shoulder seams. Sew underarm seams and sew sleeve top to armhole opening.

### NECKBAND
With 16" long circular needle and C, pick up and knit 34 (38, 38, 38, 38, 38, 42, 42) sts across back neck opening, pick up 36 (36, 36, 36, 36, 36, 44, 44) sts down left front neck edge, pick up 1 st at center front neck edge, pick up 36 (36, 36, 36, 36, 36, 44, 44) sts up right front neck edge—107 (111, 111, 111, 111, 111, 131, 131) sts.

With C, est k2, p2 ribbing as follows: (P2, k2) end p2 before center front st, k1, (p2, k2) rep to end of round.

**Next round:** Work to 1 st before center front st, VDD, work to end of round.

Rep last 2 rounds once more, then with A rep last 2 rounds twice, then with C rep last 2 rounds twice—95 (99, 99, 99, 99, 99, 119, 119) sts.

BO all sts loosely in ribbing.

Weave in ends.

## This sweater was knit with:

Knit Picks *Andean Silk*, 55% super fine alpaca, 23% silk, 22% merino wool, 96yd/87m, 1.75oz/50g per skein

(A) 3 (4, 5, 7, 8, 10, 12, 15) skeins, color 23510 Lettuce

(B) 5 (6, 8, 10, 12, 15, 18, 21) skeins, color 23515 Olive

(C) 3 (4, 5, 7, 8, 10, 12, 15) skeins, color 23511 Sangria

Chart A

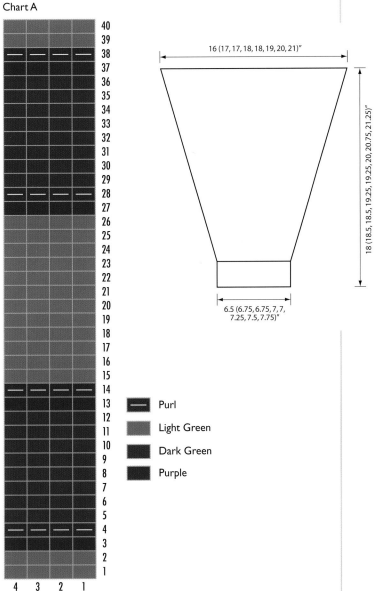

- Purl
- Light Green
- Dark Green
- Purple

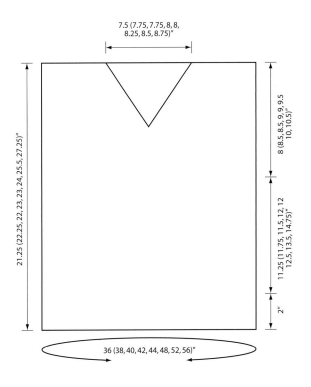

FINISHED
MEASUREMENTS
**Approx:** 10 (12)"/25.5
(30.5)cm by 14 (18)"/35.5
(45.5)cm after felting
*Exact size is determined
by felting process.*

# Pet Box Sofa

If you're tired of vacuuming pet hair off the couch, knit this doggie sofa. With any luck, he'll like the cushy knitting so much that he won't bother your furniture again. The bed is made with two-color double knitting, and then felted to form a thick, indestructible fabric.

## MATERIALS
**Approx total:** 550 (1210)yd/501 (1101)m of wool/alpaca blend bulky weight yarn and 220 (440)yd/200 (400)m wool worsted weight yarn

**Color A:** 110 (330)yd/100 (300)m in cinnamon

**Color B:** 110 (220)yd/100 (200)m in dark green

**Color C:** 330 (660)yd/300 (601)m in light green

**Color D:** 110 (220)yd/100 (200)m in pumpkin

**Color E:** 110 (220)yd/100 (200)m in yellow

## Knitting needles
6mm (Size 10 U.S.) circular needle 24"/61cm long *or size to obtain gauge*

6.5mm (Size 10 1/2 U.S.) circular needle 24"/61cm long

Darning needle for weaving in ends

## GAUGE
Approx 2 sts and 3 rows = 1"/2.5cm in Double Knitting before felting

*Exact gauge is not critical; stitches should be loose with space between them.*

# Instructions

Double Knitting is used to make this dog bed. Please refer to your swatch to see how the top and bottom edges of cushion are fashioned. See page 14 for Double Knitting instructions.

## Sides

With a strand each of A and B held together and larger needles, cast on 24 (40) sts. *Work 4 rows of Garter Stitch (knit every stitch in every row) with both strands.

**FIRST STRIPE**

**Next row:** Change to smaller needle and with Color A strand to the back of the work and Color B strand to the front, work first st as follows:

Keeping A to back and B to front, with A, knit 1 st, do not kick off of the left-hand needle. With B, purl the same st, kick st off needle. You have just knit 2 sts into 1 st. Repeat with every st on needle to end of row—48 (80) sts on needle, alternating A st, B st. At end of row turn work, do not twist yarns.

**Next row:** With B yarn to the back and A yarn to the front, work next st as follows: With B, knit next (B) st, kick st off needle. With A, purl next (A) st, kick st off needle. Cont in this manner, working A sts with A and B sts with B but keeping both strands to their own sides of the work, work across all sts.

**SECOND STRIPE**

And end of row turn work. This time do twist yarns, changing places so that A and B yarns are reversed and are opposite sides.

With back yarn knit next st, with front yarn purl next st. Cont in this manner, working A sts with B and B sts with A, keeping both strands to their own sides of the work, work across all sts. At end of row turn work; do not twist yarns.

**Next row:** Cont working the yarns on the same side they were on in the previous row, with back yarn k next st, with front yarn, p next st. Cont in this manner, working A sts with A and B sts with B, work to end of row.

Cont working in this manner, creating a double-sided pocket that is closed on one edge and open on the other. Work until piece measures 13 (17)"/33 (43)cm from start of stripe section.

**Next row:** With A and B held together, (K2tog) across—24 (40) sts on needle.

Rep from * three more times to create 4 sides in the following color combinations:

**Side 2:** Colors B and C.

**Size 3:** Colors C and A.

**Side 4:** Colors B and C.

BO all sts with larger needle loosely. Sew bound-off and cast-on edges together.

## Bottom

With a strand each of D and E held together and smaller needles, cast on 40 (50) sts. Work in garter st until piece measures 14 (18)"/35.5 (45.5)cm from cast-on edge. BO all sts. Weave in ends.

## Finishing

Felt both pieces (large double-knit piece and bed bottom) by washing them in any washing machine with a hot wash, cold rinse, and heavy-duty agitation cycle. Dry in dryer and remove pieces when still slightly damp. Hand-block to square up the pieces. If necessary, re-dampen pieces to make them more malleable.

Stuff each hollow side of the dog bed with fiberfill stuffing and sew bottom edge closed.

Turn bed inside out and sew bottom to the bottom edges of the bed, lining up corners. Turn bed right side out and invite Fido to enjoy!

MEN WHO KNIT

**Kenneth L.K. Smith**
New York City, New York

"I love the rich, natural, undyed coloring of Corriedale fleece, and spin it to make my own handspun yarns for use in my projects."

### This bed was knit with:

Knit Picks' *Sierra*, 70% wool, 30% superfine alpaca, 110yd/100m, 1.75oz/50g per skein
(A) 1 (3) skeins, color 23786 Cinnamon
(B) 1 (2) skeins, color 23787 Leaf
(C) 3 (6) skeins, color 23791 Bud

Knit Picks' *Wool of the Andes*, 100% Peruvian highland wool , 110yd/100m, 1.75oz/50g per skein
(D) 1 (2) skeins, color 23430 Pumpkin
(E) 1 (2) skeins, color 23710 Yellow

MEN WHO KNIT

## Kevin Pollard
### Wilcox, Arizona

"I grew up in a small farming town where yarn selection was limited. Now I work as a manager at World Wide Hobbie, have a wide variety of yarns at my fingertips, and teach others to knit and crochet."

SKILL LEVEL
Intermediate

FINISHED
MEASUREMENTS
**Chest:** 34 (37, 40, 42, 44,
48, 52, 56)"/86.5 (94, 101.5,
106.5, 112, 122, 132, 142)
*See Men's Sizes on page
20 for tips on choosing the
correct size.*

# Three-Color Handpaint Anorak

Made from a silk blend, bulky yarn, this heavy sweater is just waiting for a trip to the ski slopes. Knitted on large needles with very simple stitch patterns, it will work up quickly even in the largest sizes.

## MATERIALS

**Approx total:** 312 (389, 486, 608, 760, 950, 1140, 1368)yd/284 (354, 442, 553, 692, 865, 1037, 1245)m wool and silk blend bulky weight yarn

**Color A:** 213 (266, 333, 416, 520, 650, 780, 936)yd/194 (242, 303, 379, 473, 592, 710, 852)m in variegated greens and blues

**Color B:** 66 (82, 102, 128, 160, 200, 240, 288)yd/60 (75, 93, 116, 146, 182, 218, 262)m in green

**Color C:** 33 (41, 51, 64, 80, 100, 120, 144)yd/30 (37, 46, 58, 73, 91, 109, 131)m in violet

**Knitting needles**
6.5mm (Size 10 1/2 U.S.) circular needles 29"/74cm, 12"/31cm long, and double-pointed needles *or size to obtain gauge*

6mm (Size 10 U.S.) circular needles 29"/74cm long and double-pointed needles

4 stitch holders or scrap yarn

1 stitch marker

Darning needle for weaving in ends

GAUGE
3.75 sts and 4 rows = 1"/2.5cm in St st using size 6.5mm (Size 10 1/2 U.S.) needles

*Always take time to check your gauge.*

# Instructions

Body and sleeves are worked in the round to the armholes. Body and sleeves are joined at the yoke and worked in one piece to the neck.

## Body

With B and 29" long smaller needle cast on 128 (140, 152, 156, 164, 180, 196, 212) sts.

Work 4 rows of k2, p2 ribbing, then join and begin working in the round, placing marker to note start of round. Change to A and work in ribbing for 3"/7.5cm.

**Next round:** Change to larger 29" long needle and knit 1 round. Change to B and knit 1 round, then purl 3 rounds.

**SET UP STITCH PATTERN**
**Round 1:** With A, (k1, p1) rep to end of round.

**Rounds 2 through 4:** Knit.

**Repeat rounds 1 to 4** until body measures 12 (12.5, 13, 13.5, 14, 14.5, 15, 15.5)"/30.5 (32, 33, 34.5, 35.5, 37, 38, 39.5) from cast on-edge, or desired body length.

Change to B and knit 1 round, then purl 5 rounds. With A knit 3 rounds.

Divide sts evenly for front and back—64 (70, 76, 78, 82, 90, 98, 106) sts each side.

## ARMHOLE SHAPING

Working back and forth, from each armhole edge BO 4 (6, 6, 6, 6, 8, 8) sts at start of next 2 rows, then BO 3 (3, 3, 3, 4, 4, 4, 4) sts at start of next 4 rows—44 (46, 52, 54, 54, 62, 66, 74) sts rem each side. Slip sts onto holder or separate piece of yarn to work later.

# Sleeves

With A and double-pointed needles, cast on 24 (26, 28, 30, 30, 30, 32, 32) sts.

Work 4 rows of k2, p2 ribbing, then join and begin working in the round, placing marker to note start of round. Continue in ribbing for 3"/7.5cm.

**Next round:** Change to larger double-pointed needles and knit 1 round.

## SET UP STITCH PATTERN

**Round 1:** With A (k1, p1) rep to end of round.

**Rounds 2 through 4:** Knit.

**Repeat rounds 1 to 4** AND AT THE SAME TIME inc 1 st at center marker every 2 rows 32 (34, 36, 36, 38, 40, 40, 42) times, being certain to alternate inc before and after marker—56 (60, 64, 66, 68, 70, 72, 74) sts. Change to 12" long circular needle when sts no longer fit on dpns. Work even until sleeve measures 13 (14, 15.25, 15.75, 16.5, 17, 17.5, 18.25)"/33 (35.5, 38.5, 40, 42, 43, 44.5, 46.5)cm from cast-on row, or desired length.

Change to B and knit 1 round, then purl 5 rounds. With A knit 3 rounds.

## ARMHOLE SHAPING

Turn work. Working back and forth from this point on, BO 4 (6, 6, 6, 6, 6, 8, 8) sts at start of next 2 rows, then BO 3 (3, 3, 3, 4, 4, 4, 4) sts at start of next 4 rows—36 (36, 40, 42, 40, 42, 40, 42) sts rem.

# Yoke

Slip all sts onto circ needle, placing a marker between the right sleeve and back to note start of round:

36 (36, 40, 42, 40, 42, 40, 42) sts left sleeve; 44 (46, 52, 54, 54, 62, 66, 74) sts front; 36 (36, 40, 42, 40, 42, 40, 42) sts right sleeve; 44 (46, 52, 54, 54, 62, 66, 74) sts back—160 (164, 184, 192, 188, 208, 212, 232) sts total. Join to knit in the round.

With A knit one round.

**Next round:** Knit, dec 0 (4, 4, 2, 8, 8, 2, 2) sts evenly around all sts—160 (160, 180, 190, 180, 200, 210, 230) sts

Work 14 rows of Chart A Colorwork Patt as follows:

**Rounds 1 to 5:** With C, knit 1 round, then purl 4 rounds.

**Rounds 6 and 7:** With A, knit 2 rounds.

**Rounds 8 to 12:** With B, knit 1 round then purl 4 rounds.

**Round 13:** With A, knit 1 round.

**Round 14:** With A, (K8, then k2tog) 16 (16, 18, 19, 18, 20, 21, 23) times—144 (144, 162, 171, 162, 180, 189, 207) rem.

Cont in color patt as est, always working decreases in rnd 6 or 13 of patt, shape Yoke as follows, changing to shorter needles as necessary: Work 14 (14, 14, 14, 14, 14, 14, 14) rnds, then dec in next rnd (rnd 6 or 13 of chart): (K7, then k2tog) 16 (16, 18, 19, 18, 20, 21, 23) times—128 (128, 144, 152, 144, 160, 168, 184) rem.

Work 7 (7, 7, 14, 7, 14, 14, 14) rnds, then dec in next rnd (rnd 6 or 13 of patt): (K4, then k2tog) 21 (21, 24, 25, 24, 26, 28, 30) times, end k2 (2, 0, 2, 0, 4, 0, 4) —107 (107, 120, 127, 120, 134, 140, 154) rem.

Work 7 (7, 7, 7, 7, 7, 7, 7) rnds, then dec in next rnd (rnd 6 or 13 of patt): (K3, then k2tog) 21 (21, 24, 25, 24, 26, 28, 30) times, end k2 (2, 0, 2, 0, 4, 0, 4)—86 (86, 96, 102, 96, 108, 112, 124) rem.

Work 7 (7, 7, 7, 7, 7, 7, 7) rnds, then dec in next rnd (rnd 6 or 13 of patt): (K2, then k2tog) 21 (21, 24, 25, 24, 27, 28, 31) times, end k2 (2, 0, 2, 0, 0, 0, 0)—65 (65, 72, 77, 72, 81, 84, 93) rem.

Cont with A, work 2 rounds in St st, then dec in next rnd: (K2, then k2tog) 16 (16, 18, 19, 18, 20, 21, 23) times (end k1 [1, 0, 1, 0, 1, 0, 1])—49 (49, 54, 58, 54, 61, 63, 70) rem.

## NECK SHAPING

With B, work back and forth with short row shaping around rem 49 (49, 54, 58, 54, 61, 63, 70) as follows:

Starting at contrasting marker, K24 (24, 26, 28, 26, 30, 30, 34), W&T.

**Next row (WS):** P36 (36, 39, 42, 39, 45, 45, 51), W&T.

**Next row (RS):** K32 (32, 35, 38, 35, 41, 41, 47), W&T.

**Next row (WS):** P28 (28, 31, 34, 31, 37, 37, 43), W&T.

**Next round (RS):** Return to working in the round and knit next round, drawing wrap up onto needle and knitting it along with the wrapped stitch at the point of each W&T.

Knit 1 round, dec 1 (dec 1, inc 2, inc 2, inc 2, dec 1, inc 1, inc 2)—48 (48, 56, 60, 56, 60, 64, 72) sts rem.

With B, work 2, p2 ribbing for 4"/10cm, bind off all sts loosely.

## Finishing

Sew bound-off edge of neck to start of ribbing on wrong side of work. Sew small ribbing seam at cuffs and hem. Sew underarm seams. Weave in ends.

### This sweater was knit with:

Lorna's Laces *Swirl Chunky*, 85% Merino, 15% Silk, 120yd/109m, 4oz/112g per skein
(A) 1 (2, 2, 3, 4, 5, 6, 7) skeins, color 504 Lakeview
(B) 1 (1, 1, 1, 1, 1, 2, 2) skeins, color 7ns Cedar
(C) 1 (1, 1, 1, 1, 1, 1, 1) skein, color 37ns Violet Blue

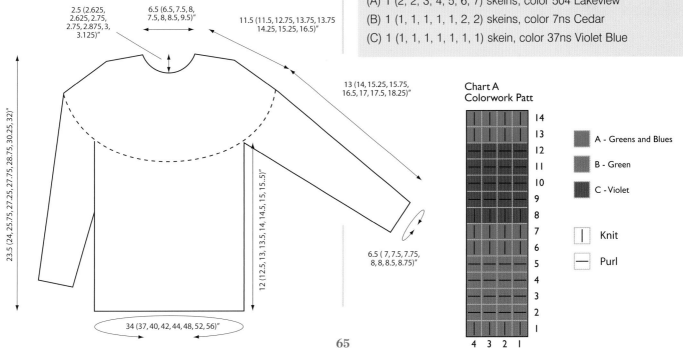

Chart A
Colorwork Patt

A - Greens and Blues
B - Green
C - Violet

| Knit
— Purl

SKILL LEVEL
Intermediate

FINISHED
MEASUREMENTS
**Girth:** 12.25 (16.5, 20.5, 24.5, 28.75, 32.75, 37, 41)"/31 (42, 52, 62, 73, 83, 94, 104)cm
*See Dog Sizes on page 20 for tips on choosing the correct size.*

MATERIALS
**Approx total:** 99 (124, 155, 195, 243, 304, 380, 456)yd/90 (113, 141, 177, 221, 277, 346, 415)m wool and silk blend bulky weight yarn

**Color A:** 39 (49, 61, 77, 96, 120, 150, 180)yd/35 (45, 56, 70, 87, 109, 137, 164)m in variegated greens

**Color B:** 39 (49, 61, 77, 96, 120, 150, 180)yd/35 (45, 56, 70, 87, 109, 137, 164)m in green

**Color C:** 21 (26, 33, 41, 51, 64, 80, 96)yd/19 (24, 30, 37, 46, 58, 73, 87)m in variegated greens and blues

# Three-Color Doggie Anorak

If your dog gets the chills easily, this heavy jacket will be his favorite winter coat. Vertical double decreases are used to shape the chest while at the same time creating a symmetrical ribbed pattern.

## GAUGE

3.75 sts and 4 rows =
1"/2.5cm in St st using 6.5mm
(Size 10 1/2 U.S.) needles

*Always take time to check
your gauge.*

**Knitting needles**
6.5mm (Size 10 1/2 U.S.)
circular needle in a length
shorter than the sweater
chest measurement, double-
pointed needles for smallest
sizes *or size to obtain gauge*

5.5mm (Size 9 U.S.) circular
needle in a length shorter than
the sweater chest measurement
and double-pointed needles

8 stitch markers
(1 in a contrasting color)

Darning needle for
weaving in ends

# Instructions

Body is worked in the round to the armholes. The chest and back are then
worked back and forth. The pieces are rejoined and the body is finished in the
round. Stitches are picked up at the armholes, and the sleeves are knit last.

## Body

With smaller circular or dpns, needle and B, cast on 20 (24, 32, 36, 44, 48, 56,
60) sts. Join to work in the round.

Work in k2, p2 ribbing for 2 (2, 4, 4, 4, 4, 6, 6) rounds, then work 2 rounds of St
st. Switch to A and work 6 more rounds in ribbing. Switch to larger needles.

**Beg 5-round stitch motif as follows:**

**Round 1:** With C, k0 (0, 2, 0, 2, 0, 0, 2) sts, (k 4 [4, 4, 6, 5, 6, 8, 8] sts, m1,
place marker) rep to end of round, end k0 (0, 2, 0, 2, 0, 0, 2)—25 (30, 39, 42, 52,
56, 63, 67) sts.

**Rounds 2 to 4:** Purl all sts.

**Round 5:** With A, knit 1 round.

Substituting color B for C, repeat 5-round patt 5 times, inc 1 st between markers
in each round 1 of pattern, staggering increases so they fall in a different place
each round.

Repeat 5-round patt 1 more time, this time working only in A—50 (60, 74, 72, 92,
96, 98, 102) sts.

**Beg 4-round stitch motif as follows:**

**Round 1:** (K1, p1) rep to end of round.

**Rounds 2 to 4:** Knit all sts.

**Rep last 4 rounds,** inc 1 st between each marker every other round 0 (0, 0, 3,
2, 3, 6, 7) times—50 (60, 74, 90, 108, 120, 140, 151) sts.

Work even until piece measures 4.25 (5.5, 7, 8.5, 9.75, 11.25, 12.5, 14)"/11 (14, 18, 21.5, 25, 28.5, 32, 35.5)cm from cast-on edge (or length to fit from dog's neck to arm comfortably). Remove all markers but one; this will be the dog's center chest.

**Next round:** Dec 2 (0, 2, 2, 0, 0, 0, 3) sts evenly around all sts in last round—48 (60, 72, 88, 108, 120, 140, 148) sts rem.

**ARMHOLE SHAPING**
Worked back and forth.

**Next row (RS):** Switch to smaller needles. Starting at marker k1, (p2, k2) rep until 8 (10, 12, 15, 17, 20, 22, 24) sts have been worked, turn.

**Next row (WS):** Work back to center marker, remove marker and cont in ribbing, work 8 (10, 12, 15, 17, 20, 22, 24) sts, turn. You have just worked 16 (20, 24, 30, 34, 40, 44, 48) sts across the center chest. The center 2 sts are knit sts when viewed from the right side.

**Next row (RS):** Working only with the center chest sts, work ribbing for 7 (9, 11, 14, 16, 19, 21, 23) sts, k2tog (creating center st), work to end—15 (19, 23, 29, 33, 39, 43, 47) sts.

**Next row (WS):** Work in ribbing patt as est.

**Next row (RS):** Work in ribbing patt as est to 1 st before center st, VDD, work to end of center chest sts in rib.

**Next row (WS):** Work in ribbing patt as est.

**Next row (RS):** Working in rib patt as est with no center decrease in this row, dec 1 st at start and end of row.

**Repeat last 4 rows** 2 (3, 4, 5, 5, 6, 7, 8) times—7 (7, 7, 9, 13, 15, 15, 15) sts rem across center chest. Work center chest sts even with no shaping until armhole measures 2.25 (3, 3.75, 4.5, 5.25, 6, 6.75, 7.5)"/5.5 (7.5, 9.5, 11.5, 13.5, 15, 17, 19)cm. Break yarn.

# Back

Reattach yarn to back. Working back and forth on back sts only, cont working in 4-row patt as est.

Work 2 rows even with no shaping, then dec 1 st at start of each row until 20 (32, 40, 42, 58, 64, 72, 76)sts rem in back section. Work even until back section is same length as center front section.

**JOINING BODY AFTER ARMHOLE**
**Next round (RS):** Work across all back sts, join with center front sts. Work to 1 st before center st, VDD, work to end of center front sts, join with back sts—27 (39, 47, 51, 71, 79, 87, 19) sts. Cont in rib patt across back sts as est in chest sts, dec at center st every other round until 23 (35, 41, 45, 65, 73, 79, 83)sts rem. Work even until piece measures 6.75 (9, 11.25, 13.5, 15.75, 18, 20.25, 22.5)"/17 (23, 28.5, 34.5, 40, 45.5, 51.5, 57)cm.

Change to C and work 2 rounds in rib. Change to B and cont in rib for 5 (6, 8, 9, 11, 12, 14, 15) more rounds. Bind off loosely in rib.

## Sleeves

With A and smaller dpns, pick up and knit 16 (24, 32, 40, 40, 48, 56, 64) sts around left armhole. Work in k2, p2 ribbing for 0.5 (0.5, 0.75, 0.75, 1, 1, 1.25, 1.5)"/1.5 (1.5, 2, 2, 2.5, 2.5, 3, 4) cm, switch to B and cont in rib for 3 rounds. Bind off all sts loosely in rib. Repeat for right armhole.

Weave in ends.

## This sweater was knit with:

Lorna's Laces *Swirl Chunky*, 85% Merino, 15% Silk, 120yd/109m, 4oz/112g per skein
(A) 1 (1, 1, 1, 1, 1, 2, 2) skeins, color 43ns Sage
(B) 1 (1, 1, 1, 1, 1, 2, 2) skeins, color 7ns Cedar
(C) 1 (1, 1, 1, 1, 1, 1, 1) skein, color 504 Lakeview

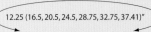

12.25 (16.5, 20.5, 24.5, 28.75, 32.75, 37.41)"

WAIST

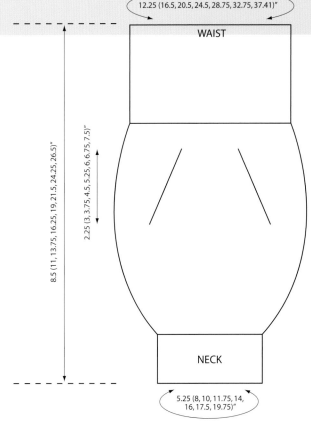

8.5 (11, 13.75, 16.25, 19, 21.5, 24.25, 26.5)"

2.25 (3, 3.75, 4.5, 5.25, 6, 6.75, 7.5)"

NECK

5.25 (8, 10, 11.75, 14, 16, 17.5, 19.75)"

# Plaid Zip Front Jacket

The plaid pattern in this jacket is made using a slip-stitch technique. It looks hard, but you'll be amazed at just how easy it really is. Your knitter friends will never figure out how you managed to knit plaid.

## MATERIALS

**Approx total:** 1440 (1800, 2160, 2592, 3107, 3732)yd/1310 (1638, 1966, 2359, 2827, 3396)m wool-cotton blend Aran weight yarn

**Color A:** 320 (400, 480, 576, 691, 829)yd/291 (364, 437, 524, 629, 754)m in marine blue

**Color B:** 240 (300, 360, 432, 518, 622)yd/218 (273, 328, 393, 471, 566)m in olive

**Color C:** 640 (800, 960, 1152, 1382, 1659)yd/582 (728, 874, 1048, 1258, 1510)m in brick

**Color D:** 240 (300, 360, 432, 518, 622)yd/218 (273, 328, 393, 471, 566)m in natural

**Knitting needles**
5mm (Size 8 U.S.) circular knitting needle at least 24"/61cm long *or size to obtain gauge*

4.5mm (Size 7 U.S.) circular knitting needle at least 24"/61cm long

4.5mm (Size 7 U.S.) circular knitting needle 12"/30.5cm long for pocket

Separating zipper, measurement TBD when sweater is finished

Sewing thread to match color A

Sewing needle

Darning needle for weaving in ends

GAUGE
4.75 sts and 10 rows = 1"/2.5cm in Chart A Plaid Patt using 5mm (Size 8 U.S.) needles

4.5 sts and 6.5 rows = 1"/2.5cm in St st using 5mm (Size 8 U.S.) needles

*Always take time to check your gauge.*

## Special Pattern Stitch
**PLAID PATTERN**

**Set-up Row (work once):** Set up each vertical stripe as designated on Chart A on page 73 by knitting across right side of work as follows: (With A k6, with B k10, with C k6, with D k10) repeat to end of row, twisting yarns at color change.

**Row 1 (RS):** Slide work to right end of circ needle and, using a single strand of CC, (k1, sl1) across work.

**Row 2 (WS):** Purl each color in its designated vertical stripe, twisting yarns at each color change.

**Row 3 (WS):** Slide work to right end of needle and, using a single strand of CC, (p1, sl1) across work.

**Row 4 (RS):** Knit each color in its designated vertical stripe.

In the above 4-row patt, 2 rows are worked on the right side, then 2 rows are worked on the wrong side (see Chart A). These four rows will result in a 2-row plaid patt.

# Instructions

Back is worked up from the hem to the armholes, then stitches are cast on for sideways knit sleeves. After working the neck, the fronts are worked down to the hem. The side and underarm sections are picked up and knit out sideways.

## Body

With larger needle, following the colors from row 1 of Chart A and using a long tail cast on, CO 76 (76, 84, 84, 96, 104) sts as follows: (CO 9 sts in C, CO 8 sts in B, CO 15 sts in A) rep to end of row, ending with st 12 (12, 20, 20, 0, 8) of chart. This counts as a RS row.

**Next row (RS):** Slip all sts back to start of needle and work this row as a RS row. With D, following row 2 of chart, (sl 1 st, k 1 st) rep to end of row, keeping D floats to WS (back) of work.

**Next row (WS):** Using A, B, and C strands as left from cast-on row and working in charted vertical stripe as established, purl across row.

**Next row (WS):** Slip all sts back to other end of needle and work this row as a WS row. With D, following row 4 of chart, (sl 1 st, p 1 st) rep to end of row, keeping D floats to WS (front) of work.

Cont in Plaid Patt as established, working 2 RS rows, then 2 WS rows by slipping sts to start of needle every other row, until back measures 12.5 (12.75, 13.25, 13.75, 14.75, 16)"/32 (32.5, 33.5, 35, 37.5, 40.5)cm.

**SLEEVE INCREASES**

Inc 2 sts at both ends of every slip stitch row until 284 (292, 300, 308, 328, 336) sts. Work even for 4 rows.

**NECK SHAPING**

Cont in patt as est, work 125 (129, 132, 136, 145, 148) sts. Join 2nd ball of yarn and BO center 34 (34, 36, 36, 38, 40) sts. Work rem 125 (129, 132, 136, 145, 148) sts, cont in patt as est. Work even for one 4-row plaid repeat.

Working both sides at once, cast on 1 (1, 1, 1, 1, 1) st at neck edge every 4th row 2 times, then CO 2 (2, 2, 2, 3, 3) sts at neck edge every other row 2 times, then CO 2 (2, 2, 2, 2, 2) sts at neck edge every row 3 times, then CO 5 (5, 6, 6, 5, 6) sts at neck edge once.

AT THE SAME TIME reverse sleeve shaping by binding off 2 sts at start of every slip stitch row until 40 (40, 44, 44, 48, 52) sts rem for each front. Cont in patt as est until fronts measure same as back. BO all sts.

Steam block, weave in ends.

# Left Side

With RS facing, and using A and larger circular needle, working along left side front, pick up 50 (51, 53, 55, 59, 64) sts from bottom edge to sleeve shaping, then pick up 67 (70, 73, 75, 79, 81) sts along underside of sleeve—117 (121, 126, 130, 138, 145) sts.

**Next row (WS):** P82 (86, 91, 95, 103, 110) sts. With a piece of waste yarn k30, slip these 30 sts back onto the left-hand needle and p to end of row (pocket opening created).

Work even in St st with A for 6 (8, 8, 10, 10, 10)"/15 (20.5, 20.5, 25.5, 25.5, 25.5)cm. BO all sts.

# Right Side

With RS facing, and using A and larger circular needle, working along right side front, pick up 67 (70, 73, 75, 79, 81) sts along underside of sleeve, then pick up 50 (51, 53, 55, 59, 64) sts along side of body—117 (121, 126, 130, 138, 145) sts.

**Next row (WS):** P5. With a piece of waste yarn k30, slip these 30 sts back onto the left-hand needle and p to end of row (pocket opening created).

Work remainder of right side as for left side.

# Finishing

Sew bound off edges of St st sections to back, matching underarm and sides.

**Tip:** You might want to pick up sts along back edge, then work these together with the underarm section using the 3-needle bind off (see page 20).

## BOTTOM RIBBING

With smaller needle, pick up 178 (186, 202, 210, 226, 242) sts along bottom edge. Work in k2, p2 ribbing for 1.5"/3.4cm.

## CUFFS

With short circular needle pick up 44 (44, 44, 44, 48, 48) sts around each cuff. Work in k2, p2 ribbing for 5"/12.5cm.

## FRONT PLACKETS

With smaller needle, pick up 76 (76, 80, 82, 88, 96) sts along right front. Work 6 rows in St st, work 1 row in Rev St st, work 6 rows in St st.

BO all sts. Fold placket to inside and sew bound-off edge to underside of front.

Repeat for left front.

## COLLAR

With smaller needle, pick up 76 (76, 80, 82, 88, 96) sts around neck edge. Work in k2, p2 ribbing for 6"/15cm.

## ZIPPER

Measure center front opening from bottom edge of ribbing to top edge of front facing. Buy a separating zipper to match yarn A color. Pin zipper in place, then baste in place and zip it up and down several times to be sure that zipper moves

### Measuring Gauge

4.75 sts x 10 rows
= 1" in sl st plaid

Space between lines = 1 four
row sl st plaid repeat

Chart A

| A - Marine Blue | B - Olive | C - Brick | D - Natural |
| A as slipped st | B as slipped st | C as slipped st | D as slipped st |

freely and the fronts meet without overlapping. Once zipper position is determined, hand sew zipper in place to wrong side of jacket, using thread to match yarn.

## POCKET

With short circular needle, pick up sts on either side of waste yarn along side front. You will have 30 loops to pick up along one edge of waste yarn and 31 along other edge—61 sts. Remove waste yarn. Work these sts in the round using circular needle to create pocket, working so that St st side faces into pocket. When pocket depth reaches bound-off edge of front placket, join end of pocket together using a 3-needle bind off and tack in place to wrong side of plaid front. Repeat for other pocket.

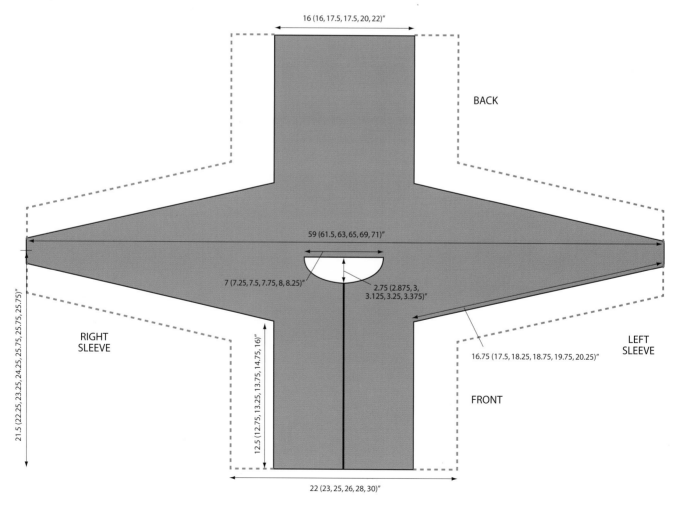

16 (16, 17.5, 17.5, 20, 22)"

BACK

59 (61.5, 63, 65, 69, 71)"

7 (7.25, 7.5, 7.75, 8, 8.25)"

2.75 (2.875, 3, 3.125, 3.25, 3.375)"

RIGHT SLEEVE

LEFT SLEEVE

21.5 (22.25, 23.25, 24.25, 25.75, 25.75, 25.75)"

12.5 (12.75, 13.25, 13.75, 14.75, 16)"

16.75 (17.5, 18.25, 18.75, 19.75, 20.25)"

FRONT

22 (23, 25, 26, 28, 30)"

# Striped Treat Bag

Instead of stashing doggie snacks in your pockets, stow them in this handy striped pouch. It's knit in the round on two circular needles and has an easy twisted cord for a drawstring strap.

# Instructions

Pouch is worked on two circular needles (see page 16).

Cast 45 sts onto one circular needle. Work 2 rows of Garter St.

Divide sts evenly between 2 circular needles—22 sts on one needle, 23 on the other. Join to knit in the round.

## Casing and facing

**Next 6 rounds:** Knit.

**Next round:** Purl.

**Next 2 rounds:** Knit.

**Next round:** K2, BO 6 sts, work to start of next needle. K2, BO 6 sts, work to end of round.

**Next round:** K2, cast on 6 sts using whatever method you prefer, work to next BO sts, CO 6, work to end of round.

**Next 2 rounds:** Knit.

## Start stripe patt

**Next 2 rounds:** With B, knit.

**Next 2 rounds:** With A, knit.

Rep last 4 rounds twice.

**Next 2 rounds:** With B, knit.

**Next 2 rounds:** With C, knit.

Rep last 4 rounds twice.

**Next 2 rounds:** With B, knit.

**Next 2 rounds:** With D, knit.

Rep last 4 rounds twice.

**Next 2 rounds:** With B, knit.

**Next 2 rounds:** With A, knit.

Rep last 4 rounds three times.

**Next round:** Purl.

## Bag Bottom

Cont with A only, dec for bottom as follows:

**Next round:** (K7, k2tog-RS) rep to end of round.

**Next round:** Knit.

**Next round:** (K6, k2tog-RS) rep to end of round.

**Next round:** Knit.

**Next round:** (K5, k2tog-RS) rep to end of round.

**Next round:** Knit.

**Next round:** (K4, k2tog-RS) rep to end of round.

**Next round:** Knit.

**Next round:** (K3, k2tog-RS) rep to end of round.

**Next round:** Knit.

**Next round:** (K2, k2tog-RS) rep to end of round.

**Next round:** Knit.

**Next round:** (K1, k2tog-RS) rep to end of round.

**Next round:** Knit.

**Next round:** (K2tog-RS) rep to end of round.

Cut yarn, leaving an 8"/20.5cm tail. Thread tail through a darning needle and draw through rem 5 sts. Pull tight to fasten off.

## Finishing

With a strand of A, stitch the first few rows together at the top of the bag.

Continuing with the same strand of yarn, turn the top facing of the bag down so that the purl row is now the top edge of the bag, and stitch the cast-on edge to the wrong side of the bag. Weave in ends.

## DRAWSTRINGS (MAKE 2)

Cut a 40"/101.5cm length of C and D. Fold each strand in half and lay the C strands over the D strands so that they form an X. Lift up the ends of the D strands and tie together in a slipknot. Repeat with the ends of the C strands so that the 2 double lengths of yarn are linked together.

Pass the D slipknot over a doorknob and hold the C slipknot in your hand. Stand far enough away from the doorknob that the yarn hangs in midair and does not touch the ground. At this point the C yarn will meet the D yarn halfway between the door and your hands.)

Slip a crochet hook into the slipknot you are holding in your hand and pull the cord taut so that the hook rests perpendicular to your fingers, allowing the strands to slip between your middle and pointer finger.

Begin turning the hook to twist the strands of yarn, similar to the way that the propeller on a toy airplane twists a rubber band. Continue twisting until the yarn is quite taut and evenly twisted. (When relaxed slightly the twisted yarn should start to kink up.)

Still holding one end of the yarn in your left hand, with your right hand pinch the twisted strand midway between yourself and the doorknob (the point where C and D meet.)

Bring the ends of the yarn together by moving toward the doorknob, but do not let go of the middle of the twisted yarn. When the 2 slipknots are together, you can release the middle of the cord. You will notice the yarn will twist around itself, forming a plied cord.

Still holding tight to the slipknot ends, loosen the yarn end from the doorknob and tie both ends together. You can run your finger between the cords to even out the twists if necessary. You can cut this cord to whatever length you want, but tie off the ends before you cut so the cord doesn't unravel.

## CREATING THE DRAWSTRING CLOSURE

Thread one drawstring through the top casing of the bag, entering at one opening and coming out the same opening. Join with a knot or wrap the ends together tightly with a piece of yarn. Repeat for the other drawstring, entering and exiting through the opening at the opposite side of the casing, and join in the same manner.

When the drawstrings are pulled, the bag will close.

This pouch was knit with:
Goddess Yarns', *Ellen*, 55% cotton, 45% wool, 81yd/74m, 1.75oz /50g per skein
(A) 1 ball in color 5621 Brick
(B) 1 ball in color 0010 Natural
(C) 1 ball in color 0514 Deep Marine
(D) 1 ball in color 0503 Olive

# Cotton Cabled Pullover with Color

Combining cables and colorwork, this sweater will keep even the most experienced knitter interested. The cotton yarn makes this a three-season garment that will become a staple in your wardrobe—even if you live where a white Christmas is only a dream.

## MATERIALS

**Approx Total:** 738 (920, 1152, 1440, 1800, 2160, 2592, 3112)yd/672 (837, 1048, 1310, 1638, 1966, 2359, 2832)m light worsted weight cotton yarn

**Color A:** 492 (614, 768, 960, 1200, 1440, 1728, 2074)yd/448 (559, 699, 874, 1092, 1370, 1572, 1887)m in red

**Color B:** 82 (102, 128, 160, 200, 240, 288, 346)yd/75 (93, 116, 146, 182, 218, 262, 315)m in yellow

**Color C:** 82 (102, 128, 160, 200, 240, 288, 346)yd/75 (93, 116, 146, 182, 218, 262, 315)m in blue

**Color D:** 82 (102, 128, 160, 200, 240, 288, 346)yd/75 (93, 116, 146, 182, 218, 262, 315)m in green

**Knitting needles**
3.75mm (Size 5 U.S.) circular needle 24"/61cm long *or size to obtain gauge*

3.75mm (Size 5 U.S.) circular needle 12"/30.5cm long and double-pointed needles

Cable needle (optional, see page 000 for instructions on cabling without a cable needle)

4 stitch holders or scrap yarn

4 stitch markers
(1 in a contrasting color)

Darning needle for sewing seams and weaving in ends

## GAUGE
6 sts and 7 rows = 1"/2.5cm in Chart B Cable Patt

5.5 sts and 6.5 rows = 1"/2.5cm in Chart A Colorwork Patt

*Always take time to check your gauge.*

# Instructions

Body and sleeves are worked in the round to the armholes. Body and sleeves are joined at the yoke and worked in one piece to the neck.

## Body

With longer circular needle and A, cast on 180 (192, 204, 216, 228, 252, 276, 300) sts. Work 4 rows in Garter Stitch (knit every row), then join to work in the round.

Beg working in Chart A Colorwork Patt, working row 1 of Chart A around all sts. Cont in charted colorwork patt as est, work to row 8 of chart. Break B, C and D.

With A, work 2 rounds of Garter Stitch (knit 1 round, purl 1 round).

Beg working in Chart B Cable Patt, working row 1 of Chart B around all sts. Cont in charted cable patt as est until body measures 12 (13.25, 14, 15, 15.5, 17, 18.25, 19.5)"/30.5 (33.5, 35.5, 38, 39.5, 43, 46.5, 49.5)cm from cast-on edge, or desired body length.

### ARMHOLE SHAPING
Divide sts evenly front and back as follows: Mark center of best-looking 6-st cable, then count 45 (48, 51, 54, 57, 63, 69, 75) sts on either side of center marker, this will be the divide for front and back—90 (96, 102, 108, 114, 126, 138, 150) sts each piece.

Working back and forth on back sts, BO 2 (2, 2, 2, 2, 6, 6, 6) sts at start of next 2 rows, then BO 2 (2, 2, 2, 2, 3, 3, 3) sts at start of next 2 rows—78 (84, 90, 96, 102, 102, 114, 126) sts rem. Rep for front. Slip sts onto holder or separate piece of yarn to work later.

## Sleeves

With dpns and A, cast on 44 (46, 50, 50, 52, 54, 56, 56) sts.

Work 4 rows in Garter St, then join to work in the round.

Beg working in Chart A Color Patt as follows: Beg with st 9 (8, 6, 6, 5, 4, 9, 9), work Chart A 3 (3, 3, 3, 3, 3, 4, 4) times around all sts. End with st 4 (5, 7, 7, 8, 9, 4, 4) of Chart A.

Cont in charted patt as est, work to row 8 of chart. Break B, C, and D.

With A, work 2 rounds of Garter St.

Beg working in Chart B Cable Patt as follows: Beg with st 1 (0, 4, 4, 12, 12, 1, 1), work Chart B 3 (3, 3, 3, 3, 3, 4, 4) times around all sts. End with st 8 (9, 5, 5, 6, 7, 8, 8) of Chart B. Working in charted cable patt, inc 1 st each edge every 6 (6, 6, 6, 4, 4, 4, 2) rows 14 (16, 17, 17, 21, 24, 26, 32) times—72 (78, 84, 84, 94, 102, 108, 120) sts. Work all incs into cable patt.

**Note:** Change to shorter circular needle when sts no longer fit on dpns.

Work even until sleeve measures 11.5 (11.75, 12.25, 13, 12.5, 13.75, 13.25, 12.25)"/29 (30, 31, 33, 32, 35, 33.5, 31)cm from cast-on edge, or desired length from underarm to cuff.

### ARMHOLE SHAPING

Working back and forth from this point, BO 4 (4, 4, 4, 4, 6, 6, 6) sts at start of next 2 rows, then BO 2 (2, 2, 2, 3, 3, 3, 3) sts at start of next 2 rows. Slip rem 56 (62, 68, 68, 74, 78, 84, 96) sts to holder.

## Yoke

Slip all sts onto longer circular needle, placing marker between each section as follows:

56 (62, 68, 68, 74, 78, 84, 96) sts left sleeve; 78 (84, 90, 96, 102, 102, 114, 126) sts front; 56 (62, 68, 68, 74, 78, 84, 96) sts right sleeve; 78 (84, 90, 96, 102, 102, 114, 126) sts back—268 (292, 316, 328, 352, 360, 396, 444) sts total. Join to knit in the round, placing contrasting color marker at end of round.

With A, k 1 round, dec 4 (4, 4, 4, 4, 0, 0, 0) sts evenly around all sts—264 (288, 312, 324, 348, 360, 396, 444) sts.

With A, p 1 round, then begin working Chart A around all sts. Work one 8-row rep of Chart A. Break B, C, and D. With A, k 1 round inc 0 (0, 0, 4, 4, 0, 4, 4) sts evenly across, then p 1 round—264 (288, 312, 328, 352, 360, 400, 448) sts.

**Next round:** With A, k76 (80, 88, 92, 96, 100, 116, 128) back sts; pm, k56 (64, 68, 72, 80, 80, 84, 96) left sleeve sts; pm, k76 (80, 88, 92, 96, 100, 116, 128) front sts; pm, k rem 56 (64, 68, 72, 80, 80, 84, 96) right sleeve sts.

With A, p 1 round, then beg working in Chart D twisted st patt around all sts and AT THE SAME TIME dec as foll at each marker: (Work to 3 sts before next marker, k2tog-LS, k1, sm, k1, k2tog-RS rep for each marker, reducing each round by 8 sts. After the first decrease round, always work the 2 sts on either side of each marker in St st.

Work the above repeat every 4th round 10 (10, 13, 12, 15, 13, 15, 18) times, changing to shorter circular needles as necessary—184 (208, 208, 232, 232, 256, 280, 304) sts rem around yoke.

Work 1 round as follows: (Work to st before next marker, remove marker, k2tog) rep for each marker. At contrasting marker, remove marker, k2tog, then slip the marker back on to mark start of round—180 (204, 204, 228, 228, 252, 276, 300) sts rem around yoke.

K 1 round, then p 1 round, removing all markers except contrasting marker if they rem at joins. Work row 1 of Chart C 15
(17, 17, 19, 19, 21, 23, 25) times around all sts. Cont in charted patt as est, working dec as marked on chart to row 36 of
chart—60 (68, 68, 76, 76, 84, 92, 100) sts rem at neck opening. Change to shorter circular needle when stitches no longer
fit on longer needle.

**NECK FACING**

**Next round:** With A, k all sts.

**Next round:** P all sts.

K 5 rounds. BO very loosely.

Fold facing at the Rev St st ridge so a row of A sits at the top
of the neck opening, and sew bound-off edge to underside
of neck.

# Finishing

Sew underarm seams.

Weave in ends.

## This sweater was knit with:

Classic Elite's *Provence*, 100% Mercerized Egyptian Cotton,
256yd/233m, 4.38 oz/125 g per skein
(A) 1 (2, 3, 3, 4, 5, 6, 8)  skeins in color 2627 French Red
(B) 1 (1, 1, 1, 1, 1, 1, 1)  skein in color 2633 Sundrenched Yellow
(C) 1 (1, 1, 1, 1, 1, 1, 1)  skein in color 2648 Slate Blue
(D) 1 (1, 1, 1, 1, 1, 1, 1)  skein in color 2615 Victory Garden

Chart A
Colorwork Band

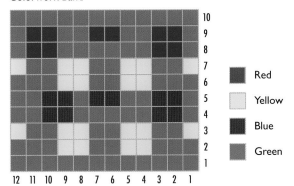

Red

Yellow

Blue

Green

Chart B
Cable Chart

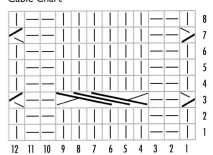

Rounds 1, 2, 4-6, 8: K1, p2, k6, p2, k1
Round 3: K1, p2, C6L, p2, TW2R (if more than 2 sts
before next repeat, otherwise k1)
Round 7: K1, p2, k6, p2, TW2R (if more than 2 sts
before next repeat, otherwise k1)

| Knit

— Purl

C6L - Cable 6 sts to twist to the left: Slip 3 and hold to front, k3, k3 slipped sts.

TW2R - Twist 2 sts to the right: K the 2nd st on LH needle, then without slipping st off needle,
K the first st on LH needle.  Slip both off needle together.

Tw2L – Take RH needle to back of work and knit 2nd st on LH needle, then without slipping
st off needle, k the first st on LH needle. Slip both off needle together.

Half of TW2R (only work when there are 2 corresponding sts at start of next repeat)

Half of TW2L (only work when there are 2 corresponding sts at end of prev repeat)

Chart D
Twist Chart

Rounds 1, 2, & 4:  P1, k2, p1
Round 3:  P1, TW2R, p1

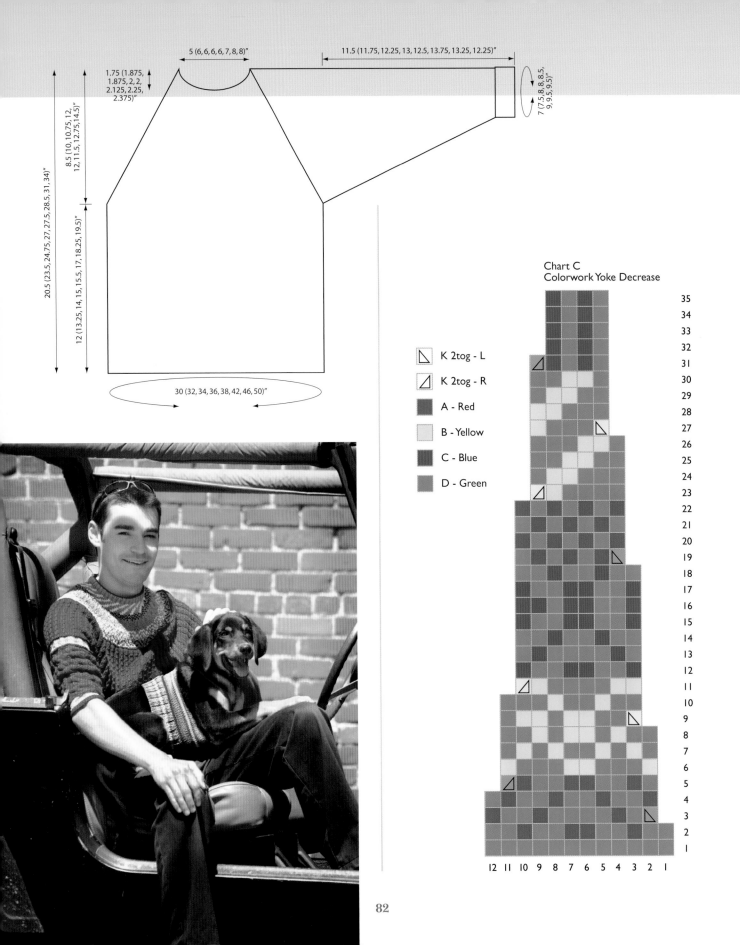

5 (6, 6, 6, 6, 7, 8, 8)"

11.5 (11.75, 12.25, 13, 12.5, 13.75, 13.25, 12.25)"

1.75 (1.875, 1.875, 2, 2, 2.125, 2.25, 2.375)"

7 (7.5, 8, 8.5, 9, 9.5, 9.5)"

8.5 (10, 10.75, 12, 12, 11.5, 12.75, 14.5)"

20.5 (23.5, 24.75, 27, 27.5, 28.5, 31, 34)"

12 (13.25, 14, 15, 15.5, 17, 18.25, 19.5)"

30 (32, 34, 36, 38, 42, 46, 50)"

## Chart C
## Colorwork Yoke Decrease

◺ K 2tog - L

◿ K 2tog - R

■ A - Red

□ B - Yellow

■ C - Blue

■ D - Green

35
34
33
32
31
30
29
28
27
26
25
24
23
22
21
20
19
18
17
16
15
14
13
12
11
10
9
8
7
6
5
4
3
2
1

12 11 10 9 8 7 6 5 4 3 2 1

FINISHED
MEASUREMENTS
**Girth:** 10.75 (15, 19, 23.25, 27.25, 31.25, 35.5, 39.5)"/27.5 (38, 48.5, 59, 69, 79.5, 90, 100.5)cm
*See Dog Sizes on page 20 for tips on choosing the correct size.*

# Fido Muscle Shirt

Whether on a leisurely stroll, or a brisk hike, your dog can show off his canine physique in this colorful Egyptian Cotton muscle shirt. The armholes and straps are self-edged with attached I-cord.

MATERIALS
**Approx Total:** 199 (275, 349, 425, 500, 575, 651, 725)yd/181 (251, 319, 388, 457, 525, 595, 662)m light worsted weight cotton yarn

**Color A:** 119 (165, 209, 255, 300, 345, 391, 435)yd/108 (150, 191, 233, 274, 315, 357, 397)m in red

**Color B:** 40 (55, 70, 85, 100, 115, 130, 145)yd/36 (50, 64, 78, 91, 105, 119, 132)m in yellow

**Color C:** 20 (28, 35, 43, 50, 58, 65, 73)yd/18 (26, 32, 39, 46, 53, 59, 67)m in blue

**Color D:** 20 (28, 35, 43, 50, 58, 65, 73)yd/18 (26, 32, 39, 46, 53, 59, 67)m in green

**Knitting needles**
4mm (Size 6 U.S.) circular needle in a length shorter than the sweater chest measurement double-pointed needles for smallest sizes *or size to obtain gauge*

3.75mm (Size 5 U.S.) circular needle in a length shorter than the sweater chest measurement double-pointed needles for smallest size

Cable needle

Stitch marker

Stitch holders

Darning needle for weaving in ends

GAUGE
4.5 sts and 6 rows = 1"/2.5cm over St st using 4mm (Size 6 U.S.) needles

*Always take time to check your gauge*

## Special Stitches

### CABLE CAST-ON (SEE PAGE 13)

Adjust work so that all sts are on the left-hand needle. Slip needle between 1st and 2nd sts on left-hand needle and pull loop through to front. Slip this loop onto the left-hand needle, twisting it clockwise. Repeat, each time using new st as new 1st stitch on left-hand needle.

### DOUBLE KNIT SLIPPED ST EDGE (DKSS)

**Row 1 (RS):** K1, wyif sl1, k1, work to last 3 sts, k1, wyif sl1, k1.

**Row 2 (WS):** Wyif sl1, k1, wyif sl1, work to last 3 sts, wyif sl1, k1, wyif sl1.

**Rep rows 1 and 2** for patt.

**Note:** on RS rows wyif means yarn to the RS of work. On WS rows wyif means yarn to the WS of work.

### I-CORD BIND OFF

Cast on 2 sts at start of row using Cable Cast-On. (K2, k2togLS, slip 3 sts from right-hand needle back onto left-hand needle, pulling yarn taut across back of work), repeat across work until 3 sts rem, k3tog-LS.

# Instructions

Body is worked in the round to armholes. Then the front, back, and straps are worked back and forth.

## Body

With smaller circular or double-pointed needles and C, cast on 48 (68, 84, 104, 124, 140, 160, 176) sts. Work in k2, p2 ribbing across all sts, join to work in the round, placing stitch marker at start of round. Work 1 more round in C.

### STRIPE PATTERN

Work stripe patt in ribbing:

With C, work 2 rounds.

With D, work 4 rounds.

With C, work 2 rounds.

With B, work 2 rounds.

With C, work 2 rounds.

With D, work 4 rounds.

Change to St st.

With C, work 2 rounds.

With A, work 2 rounds.

Change to larger needles and cont working stripe patt in St st until body measures 2.5 (4, 4.75, 6, 7, 7.75, 9.25, 10)"/6.5 (10, 12, 15, 18, 19.5, 23.5, 25.5)cm from cast-on edge. End with a color C round.

### RIGHT ARMHOLE SHAPING

Using cable cast-on method and A, cast on 3 sts at end of the left-hand needle. Using I-Cord BO method, with A BO 12 (18, 23, 28, 32, 37, 42, 47) sts. Do not bind off rem 3 I-Cord sts, but allow them to remain on the right-hand needle after last BO—36 (50, 61, 76, 92, 103, 118, 129) rem, not including 3 I-cord sts. Continuing across sweater back, with A, k14 (18, 22, 28, 32, 38, 42, 48) sts.

### LEFT ARMHOLE SHAPING

Cable cast-on as above and using I-Cord BO method, BO next 12 (18, 23, 28, 32, 37, 42, 47) sts. Do not bind off 3 I-Cord sts. Continuing across front, with A k10 (14, 16, 20, 28, 28, 34, 34) sts—13 (17, 19, 23, 31, 31, 37, 37) rem at front (including I-Cord sts), 17 (21, 25, 31, 35, 41, 45, 51) rem at back (including I-Cord sts). Slip front sts to holder and set aside.

## Back

With a strand of A, work DKSS edge as foll: (K1, wyif sl 1, k1), p1. Switch to color for stripe patt and k to 1 st before last st. Switch to A and p1, turn work and cable co 3 sts—20 (24, 28, 34, 38, 44, 48, 54) sts.

**Next row (WS):** Starting with CO sts, work DKSS edge as follows: With A (wyif sl 1, k1) twice. Switch to color for stripe patt, making sure to twist strands at WS of work between colors to prevent hole, and purl to last 4 sts. With A (k1, wyif sl 1) twice.

### BACK SHAPING

Working 4 outer sts on either side in DKSS edge in C, and working center sts in stripe patt, dec in every row as follows:

**RS Rows:** Work 4 edge sts, k2, k2tog-LS, work to end as est.

**WS Rows:** Work 4 edge sts, p2, p2tog, work to end as est.

Continue decreasing until 16 sts rem on needle (4 sts in A on either edge plus 8 center sts) AND AT SAME TIME cont in stripe patt as est until Back measures approx 1 (1.25, 1.75, 2, 2.25, 2.75, 3, 3.5)"/2.5 (3, 4.5, 5, 5.5, 7, 7.5, 9)cm from start of armhole bind off. Break B, C, and D and working only in A from this point on, divide back and create shoulder straps as follows.

### BACK STRAPS

**Next row:** K1, wyif sl 1, k1, p2, k1, wyif sl 1, k1. Join second strand of A and work next 8 sts in the same manner.

**Next row (WS):** (Wyif sl 1, k1) twice, (k1, wyif sl 1) twice. Repeat for other strap.

**Next row (RS):** K1, wyif sl 1, k1, p2, k1, wyif sl 1, k1. Rep for other strap.

Cont in this manner, working both straps at the same time until straps measure 3.75 (5, 6.5, 7.75, 9.25, 10.75, 12, 13.5)"/9.5, 12.5, 16.5, 19.5, 23.5, 27.5 30.5, 34.5)cm. Slip strap sts to holder and set aside.

## Front

Slip front sts to larger needle.

**Next row (RS):** With a strand of A work 4 edge sts as follows: (K1, wyif sl 1, k1), p1. K to last st, p1, turn work and cable co 3 sts—16 (20, 22, 26, 34, 34, 40, 40) sts.

**Next row (WS):** Starting with new sts, work 4 st edge as follows: (Wyif sl 1, k1) twice. P to last 4 sts, (k1, wyif sl 1) twice.

**Next row (RS):** K1, wyif sl 1, k1, p1, k2, k2tog-LS, work to last 4 sts, p1, k1, wyif sl 1, k1.

**Next row (WS):** (Wyif sl 1, k1) twice, p2, p2tog, p to last 4 sts, (k1, wyif sl 1) twice.

Rep last 2 rows until 16 sts rem. End with a WS row.

## Finishing

Measure top on dog to make sure straps are the correct length for a comfortable fit (not too tight or too loose). Slip strap sts from holder onto smaller needle and using a larger needle as the 3rd needle, work a 3-needle bind off with the back sts and the front sts, matching the strap edges to the front sts rem. Weave in ends. Block.

**This sweater was knit with:**

Classic Elite's *Provence*, 100% Mercerized Egyptian Cotton, 256yd/233m, 4.38oz/125g per skein

(A) 1 (1, 1, 1, 1, 2, 2)  skein in color 2627 French Red
(B) 1 (1, 1, 1, 1, 1, 1)  skein in color 2633 Sundrenched Yellow
(C) 1 (1, 1, 1, 1, 1, 1)  skein in color 2648 Slate Blue
(D) 1 (1, 1, 1, 1, 1, 1)  skein in color 2615 Victory Garden

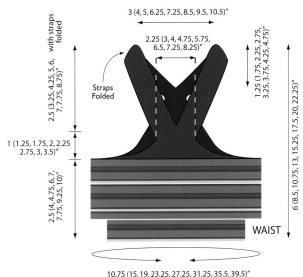

FINISHED
MEASUREMENTS
**Chest:** 32 (36, 40, 44, 48,
52, 56, 60)"/81.5 (91.5, 101.5,
112, 122, 132, 142, 152.5)cm
*See Men's Sizes on page
20 for tips on choosing the
correct size.*

# Faupi Lopi Cardigan

The body of this cardigan is knitted back and forth, but to save
you from having to purl with multiple colors, the yoke is knitted
in the round. You cut it open (gasp!) after the knitting is complete
and finish the sweater off with a zipper. This complex project is
recommended for experienced knitters.

## MATERIALS
**Approx total:** 911 (1139,
1424, 1780, 2136, 2563, 3076,
3691)yd/829 (1036, 1296,
1620, 1944, 2332, 2799,
3359)m merino wool
worsted weight yarn

**Color A:** 512 (640, 800, 1000,
1200, 1440, 1728, 2074)yd/466
(582, 728, 910, 1092, 1310,
1572, 1887)m in off white

**Color B:** 205 (256, 320, 400,
480, 576, 691, 829)yd/187
(233, 291, 364, 437, 524, 629,
754)m in blue

**Color C:** 102 (128, 160, 200,
240, 288, 346, 415)yd/93 (116,
146, 182, 218, 262, 315,
378)m in tan

**Color D:** 92 (115, 144, 180,
216, 259, 311, 373)yd/84 (105,
131, 164, 197, 236, 283,
339)m in green

## Knitting needles
3.75mm (Size 5 U.S.) circular
needle at least 29"/74cm long
*or size to obtain gauge for
St st section*

3.75mm (Size 5 U.S.) circular
needle 16"/41cm long

4.5mm (Size 7 U.S.) circular
needle at least 29"/74cm long
*or size to obtain gauge for
cable section*

Separating zipper approx 25
(27, 28.5, 30, 31, 33.25, 34.75,
37)"/63.5 (68.5, 72.5, 76, 79,
84.5, 88.5, 94)cm

Sewing needle and
thread for sewing zipper

2 stitch markers

4 stitch holders or scrap yarn

Darning needle for sewing
seams and weaving in ends

## GAUGE
5.5 sts and 6.5 rows =
1"/2.5cm in Chart A Colorwork
Patt using 3.75mm (Size 5
U.S.) needles

5.5 sts and 6.5 rows =
1"/2.5cm in Chart B Cable
Patt using 4.5mm
(Size 7 U.S.) needles

# Instructions
Body and sleeves are worked back and forth to the armholes.
The pieces are joined and the yoke is worked in the round
and steeked afterwards.

## Body
With smaller 29" long circular needle and A, cast on 184 (196,
220, 248, 260, 288, 312, 340) sts. Work in k2, p2 ribbing for 3
(3.25, 3.25, 3.5, 3.5, 3.75, 3.75, 4)"/7.5 (8.5, 8.5, 9, 9, 9.5, 9.5,
10)cm, then inc 3 (4, 6, 4, 5, 3, 5, 3) sts evenly across—187
(200, 226, 252, 265, 291, 317, 343) sts rem.

### BEG CABLE PAT
**Note:** It make be necessary to move up a needle size when
working cable patt. Check your St st and cable swatches to
see how the gauge measured across St st areas compares to
the cabled areas and adjust accordingly.

**Next row (RS):** Work all sts of Chart B 14 (15, 17, 19, 20, 22,
24, 26) times to last 5 sts, then work sts 1 to 5 once more.
Cont in charted cable patt as est until body measures 12
(13.5, 14.75, 16, 17.25, 18.75, 20, 21.5)"/30.5 (34.5, 37.5, 40.5,
44, 47.5, 51, 54.5)cm from cast-on edge, or desired body
length. End with a WS row, dec 3 (4, 6, 4, 5, 3, 5, 3) sts evenly
across— 182 (195, 221, 247, 260, 286, 312, 338) sts rem.

### DIVIDE FRONTS AND BACK AT ARMHOLES
**Next row (RS):** K 46 (49, 55, 62, 65, 72, 78, 85) sts for right
front, pm, k90 (97, 111, 123, 130, 142, 156, 168) sts for back,
pm, k46 (49, 55, 62, 65, 72, 78, 85) sts for left front.

**Next row (WS):** Purl all sts, slipping markers. Each marker
denotes an armhole edge.

## ARMHOLE SHAPING

Working each section separately in St st, BO 6 (8, 8, 8, 8, 12, 12, 14) sts at start of each armhole edge once, then BO 3 (5, 5, 5, 5, 6, 6, 8) sts at start of each armhole edge twice—34 (31, 37, 44, 47, 48, 54, 55) sts rem each front, 66 (61, 75, 87, 94, 94, 108, 108) sts rem at back.

Work 2 more rows of St st in each section. Slip sts onto holders or separate pieces of yarn to work later.

## Sleeves (make 2)

With smaller needle and A, cast on 40 (42, 46, 46, 48, 50, 50, 52) sts. Work 24 rows of k1, p1 ribbing.

### BEG CHARTED CABLE PATT

Beg with st 13 (12, 10, 10, 9, 8, 8, 1), work Chart B 3 (3, 3, 3, 3, 3, 3, 4) times around all sts, end with st 13 (2, 4, 4, 5, 6, 6, 13) of Chart B.

Working in charted cable patt, inc 1 st on either side of marker every 8 (8, 6, 6, 6, 4, 4, 4) rows 14 (15, 18, 23, 24, 28, 33, 37) times—68 (72, 82, 92, 96, 106, 116, 126) sts working inc sts into cable patt.

Work even until sleeve measures 16.25 (17.5, 18.5, 19.25, 19.75, 20.25, 20.75, 21.5)"/41.5 (44.5, 47, 49, 50, 51.5, 52.5, 54.5)cm from cast-on row, or desired length. End with a WS row.

### ARMHOLE SHAPING

Change to St st. BO 7 (10, 10, 10, 10, 14, 14, 17) sts at start of next 2 rows—54 (52, 62, 72, 76, 78, 88, 92) sts rem.

Work 2 more rows of St st in each section. Slip sts onto holders or separate pieces of yarn to work later.

## Yoke

**Note:** Worked in the round to be steeked later. Yoke can be worked back and forth if desired.

Slip all sts onto larger 29" long circular needle, placing a marker between the right sleeve and back to note start of round:

54 (52, 62, 72, 76, 78, 88, 92) sts left sleeve; 34 (31, 37, 44, 47, 48, 54, 55) sts left front; 34 (31, 37, 44, 47, 48, 54, 55) sts right front; 54 (52, 62, 72, 76, 78, 88, 92) sts right sleeve; 66 (61, 75, 87, 94, 94, 108, 108) sts back—242 (227, 273, 319, 340, 346, 392, 402) sts total. Join to knit in the round.

With B, knit all sts, inc 5 (inc 7, dec 0, inc 6, dec 2, inc 5, dec 2, inc 1) sts evenly around work—247 (234, 273, 325, 338, 351, 390, 403) sts rem. Rep round 1 of Chart A Colorwork Patt 19 (18, 21, 25, 26, 27, 30, 31) times around all sts. Cont working in chart as est, making dec where specified in chart. Work through row 66 (68, 69, 69, 68, 71, 73, 76) rows of chart—76 (72, 84, 100, 104, 81, 90, 93) sts rem.

Change to shorter circular needle when sts no longer fit on longer needle.

Sizes 32 (36, 40, 44, 48) only: With B (k2, k2tog) rep around all sts—57 (54, 63, 75, 78, 81, 90, 93) sts rem.

Sizes 52 (56, 60) only: With B, k 1 round.

**All Sizes:** With B, purl 1 round.

## NECK SHAPING

With D and starting at contrasting marker, work
4 short rows of back neck shaping as follows:

**Row 1 (RS):** K29 (26, 32, 38, 39, 41, 45,
47)sts, W&T.

**Next row (WS):** P43 (38, 47, 56, 59, 61, 68,
70)sts, W&T.

**Next row (RS):** K39 (34, 43, 52, 55, 57, 64,
66)sts, W&T.

**Next row (WS):** P35 (30, 39, 48, 51, 53, 60,
62)sts, W&T.

**Next round (RS):** Return to working in the round
and knit next round, drawing wrap up onto needle
and knitting it along with the wrapped stitch at the
point of each W&T.

## RIBBED NECKBAND

With A and smaller 16" long circular needle, knit all
sts in round, dec 3 (4, 3, 3, 4, 3, 4, 3) sts evenly
around work—54 (50, 60, 72, 74, 78, 86, 90) sts rem.

**Next round:** (K1, p1) rep around.

Cont in k1, p1 ribbing until neckband measures
1.5"/4cm. BO all sts loosely in rib.

# Finishing

Sew underarm seams and underarm openings.

## STEEKING

With a darning needle and contrasting yarn, mark
center front of yoke of sweater. With a sewing
machine stitch .25"/.5cm on either side of contrasting
yarn, creating a .50"/1.5cm "gutter" in yoke area only.
Take a deep breath. Cut down center front yoke.

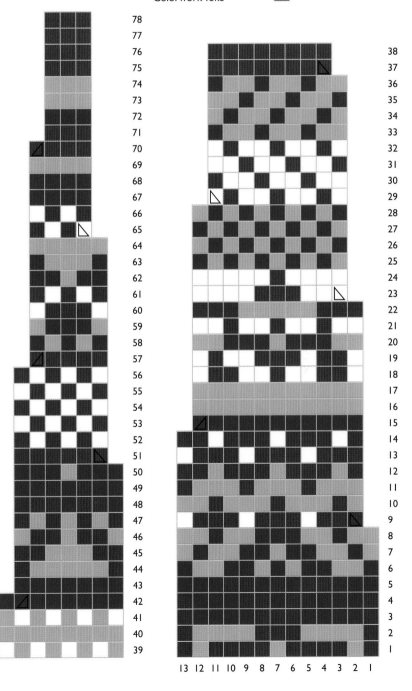

Chart A
Colorwork Yoke

Legend:
- ◿ K2 tog - R
- ◺ K2 tog - L
- ▢ A - Off White
- ■ B - Blue
- ▨ C - Tan
- ■ D - Green

## FRONT PLACKETS

With RS facing, smaller needles, and B, pick up and knit 110 (119, 125, 132, 136, 146, 153, 163) sts down left front edge from top of ribbing to bottom edge of sweater.

**Next row (WS):** With B, knit.

**Next 2 rows:** With C, knit.

**Next 2 rows:** With D, knit.

BO all sts loosely with larger needle.

Measure the center front placket and purchase a zipper 1"/2.5cm shorter than total measurement. Position zipper so that it is 1/2"/1.5cm from the top and bottom edges of placket, and pin in place. Machine or hand sew zipper in place.

Sew underarm seams. Weave in ends.

## This sweater was knit with:

Kraemer Yarns' *Summit Hill*, 100% merino superwash wool, 230 yds/209m, 3.5 oz/100g per skein
(A) 2 (2, 3, 4, 5, 6, 7, 9) skeins, color Pearl
(B) 1 (1, 1, 1, 2, 2, 3, 3) skeins, color Cadet Blue
(C) 1 (1, 1, 1, 2, 2, 2, 2) skeins, color Tan
(D) 1 (1, 1, 1, 1, 2, 2, 2) skeins, color Adventurine

**Chart B
Cables**

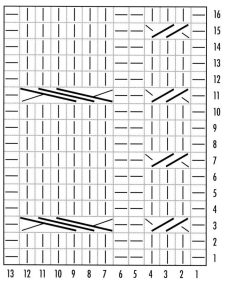

 C3R - Cable 3 sts to the right (1/2).

C6L - Cable 6 sts to the left (3/3).

| Knit on RS, purl on WS

— Purl on RS, knit on WS

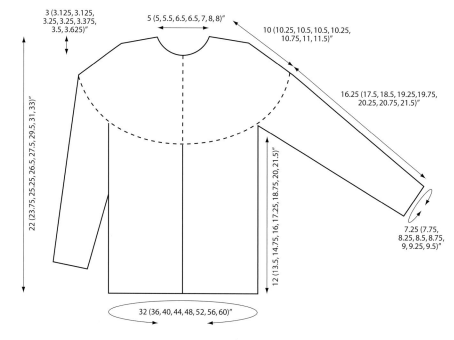

3 (3.125, 3.125, 3.25, 3.25, 3.375, 3.5, 3.625)"

5 (5, 5.5, 6.5, 6.5, 7, 8, 8)"

10 (10.25, 10.5, 10.5, 10.25, 10.75, 11, 11.5)"

16.25 (17.5, 18.5, 19.25, 19.75, 20.25, 20.75, 21.5)"

22 (23.75, 25.25, 26.5, 27.5, 29.5, 31, 33)"

12 (13.5, 14.75, 16, 17.25, 18.75, 20, 21.5)"

7.25 (7.75, 8.25, 8.5, 8.75, 9, 9.25, 9.5)"

32 (36, 40, 44, 48, 52, 56, 60)"

**SKILL LEVEL**
Intermediate

**FINISHED
MEASUREMENTS**
Approx 27"/68.5cm square

# Mitered
# Dog Blanket

Modular knitting is addictive. Block by block, the knitting grows. You'll find you want to finish one more square...then one more tier, until before you know it, you're done! You attach the squares and weave in the ends as you go, so there is almost no finishing.

**MATERIALS**
**Approx total:**
1150yd/1047m merino wool worsted weight yarn

**Color A:** 460yd/419m in blue

**Color B:** 230yd/209m in tan

**Color C:** 460yd/419m in green

**Knitting needles**
4.5mm (Size 7 U.S.)

Tapestry needle for
weaving in ends

GAUGE
Each diamond = approx
3"/7.5cm across

*Always take time to check
your gauge.*

# Instructions

Blanket is made out of tiers of mitered diamonds that are attached as you go after the first tier.

Note: Weaving in ends is a bore, but you can wrap the tails around the working yarn as you start a new color and reduce the final amount of ends to weave in. Experiment with this; it will become easier as you work through your diamonds.

## Tier 1

2-color Mitered Diamonds (make 8)

**Row 1:** With A, cast on 19 sts.

**Next row (WS):** K9 sts, p1, k to end.

**Next row (RS):** With B, k8, VDD, k to end.

**Next row (WS):** K8, p1, k to end.

**Next row (RS):** With A, k to 1 st before center st, VDD, k to end.

**Next row (WS):** K to center st, p1, k to end.

**Repeat last 2 rows** until 9 sts rem on needle, change to B.

Cont working as est until no sts rem. Fasten off.

## Tier 2

Join these diamonds together with C by picking up and knitting 10 sts along the left edge of one diamond. Working on the same needle, continuing with C, pick up and knit 10 sts along the right edge of the next diamond.

**Next row (WS):** K9, p2tog, k to end.

**Next row (RS):** With B, k to 1 st before center st, VDD, k to end.

**Next row (WS):** K to center st, p1, k to end.

**Next row (RS:)** With C, k to 1 st before center st, VDD, k to end.

**Next row (WS:)** K to center st, p1, k to end.

**Repeat last 2 rows** until 9 sts rem on needle, change to B.

Cont working as est until no sts rem. Fasten off.

Join all original diamonds in this way, creating 7 new diamonds in the process.

### TIER 2 RIGHT-EDGE DIAMOND

Create a diamond at the right edge of the blanket as follows:

With A, cast on 10 sts, then pick up and knit 10 sts along the right edge of the right-most first-tier diamond.

**Next row (WS):** K9, p2tog, k to end.

**Next row (RS):** With B, k to 1 st before center st, VDD, k to end.

**Next row (WS):** K to center st, p1, k to end.

**Next row (RS):** With A, k to 1 st before center st, VDD, k to end.

**Next row (WS):** K to center st, p1, k to end.

Repeat last 2 rows until 9 sts rem on needle, change to B.

Cont working as est until no sts rem. Fasten off.

### TIER 2 LEFT EDGE DIAMOND

Create a diamond at the left edge of the blanket as follows:

With A, pick up and knit 10 sts along the left edge of the left-most first-row diamond, then using the cable-cast on method, cast on 10 sts.

**Next row (WS):** K9, p2tog, k to end.

**Next row (RS):** With B, k to 1 st before center st, VDD, k to end.

**Next row (WS):** K to center st, p1, k to end.

**Next row (RS):** With A, k to 1 st before center st, VDD, k to end.

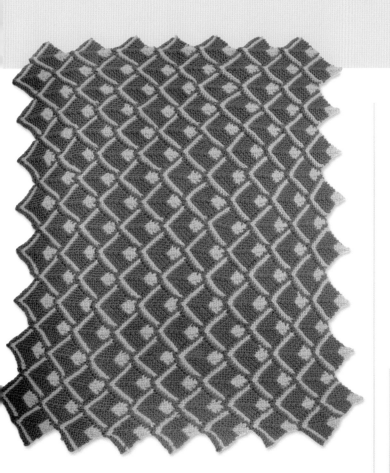

**Next row (WS):** K to center st, p1, k to end.

**Repeat last 2 rows** until 9 sts rem on needle, change to B.

Cont working as est until no sts rem. Fasten off.

## Tier 3

Create 8 new diamonds in colors A and B, nesting these in the V spaces between the diamonds in the second row. Do not create edge diamonds in this row.

Repeat Tiers 2 and 3 of diamonds until a total of 15 tiers are worked—ending with a row of 8 diamonds in B and C.

Weave in remaining ends.

### This blanket was knit with

Kraemer Yarns' *Summit Hill*, 100% merino superwash wool, 230 yds/209m, 3 1/2oz/100g per skein
(A) 2 skeins, color Cadet Blue
(B) 1 skein, color Tan
(C) 2 skeins, color Adventurine

MEN WHO KNIT

### Lawrence Joseph
New York City, New York

"I'm always looking at things and wondering how they will translate into a knitted item, whether it's a pattern repeating on a building, or the structure of a shirt, jacket, or coat."

# Doggie Fair Isle

Made to match the Fair Isle Hat on page 98, this dog sweater is a good project for practicing knitting in the round on two circular needles. For the larger sizes, you may find that a single circular needle is easier to handle. But on the small sizes, the two circulars technique is a lifesaver for those who hate double-pointed needles.

## MATERIALS

**Approx total:** 121 (155, 192, 240, 288, 347, 414, 498)yd/110 (141, 175, 218, 262, 316, 377, 453)m Aran weight alpaca yarn

**Color A:** 20 (26, 32, 40, 48, 58, 69, 83)yd/18 (24, 29, 36, 44, 53, 63, 76)m brown

**Color B:** 20 (26, 32, 40, 48, 58, 69, 83)yd/18 (24, 29, 36, 44, 53, 63, 76)m gold

**Color C:** 26 (32, 40, 50, 60, 72, 86, 104)yd/24 (29, 36, 46, 55, 66, 78, 95)m red

**Color D:** 15 (19, 24, 30, 36, 43, 52, 62)yd/14 (17, 22, 27, 33, 39, 47, 56)m blue

**Color E:** 20 (26, 32, 40, 48, 58, 69, 83)yd/18 (24, 29, 36, 44, 53, 63, 76)m dark green

**Color F:** 20 (26, 32, 40, 48, 58, 69, 83)yd/18 (24, 29, 36, 44, 53, 63, 76)m purple

**Knitting needles**
4.5mm (Size 7 U.S.) circular needle in a length shorter than the sweater chest measurement, double-pointed needles for smallest sizes *or size to obtain gauge*

4mm (Size 6 U.S.) circular needle in a length shorter than the sweater chest measurement and double-pointed needles

Tapestry needle for weaving in ends

**GAUGE**
6 sts and 7 rows = 1"/2.5cm in St st using 4.5mm (Size 7 U.S.) needles

*Always take time to check your gauge.*

# Instructions

Sweater is knitted in the round using dpns or 2 circular needles (see page 17). Armhole openings are made by knitting with waste yarn that is removed after the body is complete. Sleeves are knit last.

## Body

With smaller circular or double-pointed needles and 1 strand each of A and C held together, working a long tail cast on using C as the tail and A as the live end, cast on 24 (32, 40, 48, 56, 64, 72, 80) sts. Break C and join to work in the round.

### NECK

With A, work in k2, p2 ribbing for 1 (1.25, 1.5, 1.75, 2, 2.5, 2.75, 3)"/ 2.5 (3, 4, 4.5, 5, 6.5, 7, 7.5) cm, then work 2 rounds of Garter St.

### YOKE COLORWORK

Switch to larger needles and work row 1 of Chart A 6 (8, 10, 12, 14, 16, 18, 20) times around all sts.

Cont in chart as est, work inc as marked and changing colors as directed—72 (96, 120, 144, 168, 192, 216, 240) sts.

Work to row 21 (21, 21, 21, 30, 30, 30, 30) of chart. Look at the work to determine which is the best-looking side; this will be the back. Place marker in what will be the center of dogs chest to note start of rounds.

Continue working in St st with C and AT THE SAME TIME, work until piece measures 4.75 (6.5, 8, 9.5, 11.25, 12.75, 14.5, 16)"/12 (16.5, 20.5, 24, 28.5, 32.5, 37, 40.5)cm from cast on-edge (or length to fit from dogs neck to arm comfortably).

## ARMHOLE SHAPING

Starting at marker, work 9 (12, 15, 17, 20, 24, 26, 29) sts, with a piece of waste yarn, k6 (8, 10, 12, 14, 16, 18, 20) sts, slip these sts back onto the left-hand needle and knit them with A. Continue working around until there are 15 (20, 25, 29, 34, 40, 44, 49) sts before marker, with a piece of waste yarn, k6 (8, 10, 12, 14, 16, 18, 20) sts, slip these sts back onto the left-hand needle and knit them with A, continue in A to marker.

Work even in A with no shaping for 0 (0.5, 0.5, 1, 1, 2, 2, 3)"/0 (1.5, 1.5, 2.5, 2.5, 5, 5, 7.5)cm.

## BOTTOM COLORWORK

Work row 1 of Chart B 6 (8, 10, 12, 14, 16, 18, 20) times around all sts. Continue in charted patt as est to row 7 (7, 7, 7, 10, 10, 10, 10). Switch to smaller needles and E and begin working in k2, p2 ribbing for 2 (2, 3, 6, 9, 9, 12, 15) rounds, then switch to D and continue in ribbing for 2 (2, 3, 6, 9, 9, 12, 15) rounds. Bind off in ribbing with A.

# Sleeves

With dpns and F, pick up 7 (9, 11, 13, 15, 17, 19, 21) sts in row above right armhole waste yarn and 6 (8, 10, 12, 14, 16, 18, 20) sts in row below waste yarn. Pick up an extra 2 sts on either side of armhole—17 (21, 25, 29, 33, 37, 41, 45) sts.

Remove waste yarn. Using dpns or 2 circulars, work 1 round of armhole sts, dec 1 st—16 (20, 24, 28, 32, 36, 40, 44) sts rem. Work in k2, p2 ribbing for 6 (8, 10, 10, 12, 16, 16, 18) rounds, then switch to B and work 2 more rounds of ribbing. BO all sts loosely in B.

Weave in ends.

This sweater was knit with:

Goddess Yarns' *Phoebe*, 100% baby alpaca, (73yd/66m, 1.75oz/50g per skein

(A) 1 (1, 1, 1, 1, 1, 2, 2) skein, color 0044 Bark
(B) 1 (1, 1, 1, 1, 1, 1, 1) skein, color 8325 Fern
(C) 1 (1, 1, 1, 1, 1, 1, 1) skein, color 0178 Bittersweet
(D) 1 (1, 1, 1, 1, 1, 1, 1) skein, color 0975 Midnight
(E) 1 (1, 1, 1, 1, 1, 1, 1) skein, color A895 Willow
(F) 1 (1, 1, 1, 1, 1, 1, 1) skein, color 8126 Wild Aster

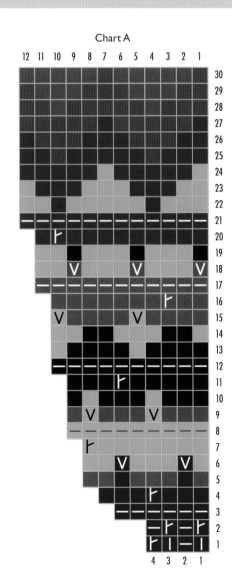

Chart A

## Chart B

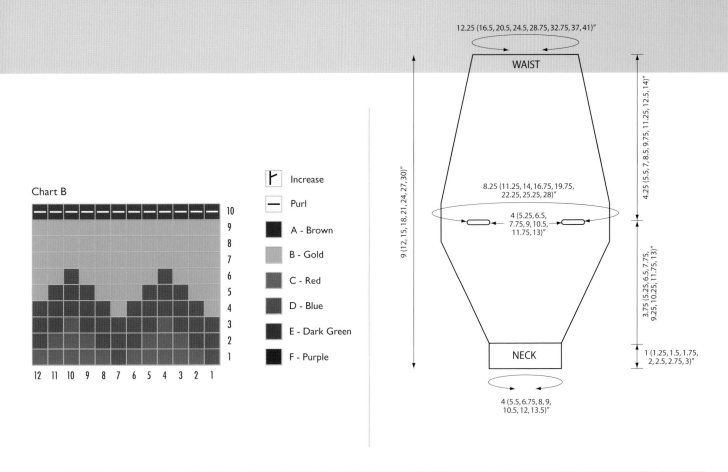

| Symbol | Meaning |
|--------|---------|
| ⌐ | Increase |
| — | Purl |
| ■ | A - Brown |
| ■ | B - Gold |
| ■ | C - Red |
| ■ | D - Blue |
| ■ | E - Dark Green |
| ■ | F - Purple |

WAIST
12.25 (16.5, 20.5, 24.5, 28.75, 32.75, 37, 41)"

4.25 (5.5, 7, 8.5, 9.75, 11.25, 12.5, 14)"

9 (12, 15, 18, 21, 24, 27, 30)"

8.25 (11.25, 14, 16.75, 19.75, 22.25, 25.25, 28)"

4 (5.25, 6.5, 7.75, 9, 10.5, 11.75, 13)"

3.75 (5.25, 6.5, 7.75, 9.25, 10.25, 11.75, 13)"

NECK

1 (1.25, 1.5, 1.75, 2, 2.5, 2.75, 3)"

4 (5.5, 6.75, 8, 9, 10.5, 12, 13.5)"

97

# Fair Isle Hat

Use this hat to practice knitting in the round on two circular needles. It's a fast technique that's easy to learn. Make the matching Doggie Fair Isle sweater on page 94, and you'll be an expert by the time you're done.

## MATERIALS
**Approx total:** 121 (152, 190, 228, 267)yd/110 (138, 173, 207, 243)m alpaca Aran weight yarn

**Color A:** 26 (32, 40, 48, 58)yd/24 (29, 36, 44, 53)m in brown

**Color B:** 19 (24, 30, 36, 43)yd/17 (22, 27, 33, 39)m in gold

**Color C:** 19 (24, 30, 36, 43)yd/17 (22, 27, 33, 39)m in red

**Color D:** 19 (24, 30, 36, 43)yd/17 (22, 27, 33, 39)m in blue

**Color E:** 19 (24, 30, 36, 43)yd/17 (22, 27, 33, 39)m in dark green

**Color F:** 19 (24, 30, 36, 43)yd/17 (22, 27, 33, 39)m in purple

**Knitting needles**
4.5mm (Size 7 U.S.) 2 circular needles 12"/30.5cm long or double-pointed needles *or size to obtain gauge*

6 stitch markers
(1 in a contrasting color)

Darning needle for weaving in ends

GAUGE
4 sts and 6 rows =
1"/2.5cm in St st

*Always take time to check your gauge.*

# Instructions
Hat is knit in the round from the top down using double-pointed needles or 2 circular needles (see page 17).

## Crown
With A, cast on 6 sts.

**Next row:** K1, m1 into each st—12 sts.

**Next row:** Purl all sts.

**Next row:** K1, m1 into each st—24 sts.

**Next row:** Purl all sts.

**Next round:** Working with dpns or 2 circs, k4, place marker (pm), rep to end of round. Place contrasting marker at end of round and join.

**SPIRAL PATT**
**Next round:** (Work to 1 st before marker, M1) rep to end of round—30 sts.

Rep last round until there are 72 (78, 84 ,90, 96) sts. Remove all markers but contrasting marker.

## COLORWORK SIDEBAND

Begin colorwork pattern, repeating Chart A 12 (13, 14 ,15, 16) times around all sts.

Work to round 25 of chart (entire round in yarn C). Repeat round twenty-five 2 (2, 3 ,3, 3) times, then continue to the end of the chart.

# Brim

**Next round:** Cont in B, inc 0 (2, 0, 2, 0) sts evenly around sts—72 (80, 84 ,92, 96) sts.

Beg working in k2, p2 ribbing. Cont in ribbing for 6 rounds, or until hat is desired length. Bind off all sts loosely in ribbing.

Sew seam at top of crown.

Steam block, weave in ends.

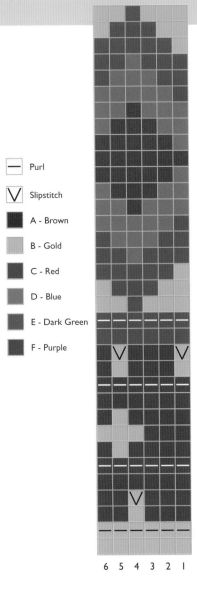

| | |
|---|---|
| — | Purl |
| V | Slipstitch |
| ■ | A - Brown |
| ■ | B - Gold |
| ■ | C - Red |
| ■ | D - Blue |
| ■ | E - Dark Green |
| ■ | F - Purple |

6 5 4 3 2 1

## This hat was knit with:

Goddess Yarns' *Phoebe*, 100% baby alpaca,
73yd/66m, 1.75oz/50g per skein
(A) 1 (1, 1, 1, 1) skein, color 0044 Bark
(B) 1 (1, 1, 1, 1) skein, color 8325 Fern
(C) 1 (1, 1, 1, 1) skein, color 0178 Bittersweet
(D) 1 (1, 1, 1, 1) skein, color 0975 Midnight
(E) 1 (1, 1, 1, 1) skein, color A895 Willow
(F) 1 (1, 1, 1, 1) skein, color 8126 Wild Aster

# Double-Knit Hemp Leash

Utilitarian yet stylish, this leash resembles a very long piece
of I-cord, but the double-knitting technique combined with
the choice of hemp yarn makes for a very strong dog lead.

# Instructions

This leash is made with Double Knitting. See page 14 for instructions on this technique.

## Leash

With a strand of A, cast on 4 (8) sts. Work in Garter Stitch (knit every row) for 6"/15cm.

**START DOUBLE KNIT REV ST ST SECTION**

**Next row:** M1 in each st—8 (16) sts.

**Next row:** (P1, sl 1) rep to end of row, end sl 1.

**Rep last row** for 4"/10cm.

**START DOUBLE KNIT ST ST SECTION**

**Next row:** (K1, wyif sl 1) rep to end of row, end wyif sl 1.

Rep last row for 2"/5cm.

Change to B and cont in Double Knit St st as est until leash is desired length. Switch to A and work 8 rows in Double Knit St st.

## Handle

Return to Double Knit Rev St st ([P1, sl 1] rep to end of row, end sl 1) until handle length is long enough to wrap around your hand comfortably with a little extra (approx 8 to 10"/20.5 to 25.5cm). BO all sts.

## Finishing

Sew bound-off edge to start of handle very tightly.

Slip bold snap onto other end of leash and fold cast-on edge up. Sew very securely in place (you may want to machine-sew this with heavy thread for a strong dog.)

This leash was knit with:

Lana Knits' *All Hemp 6*, 100% hemp, 150 yd/137m, 3.25oz/91g per skein
(A) 1 skein, color Avocado
(B) 1 skein, color Deep Sea

MEN WHO KNIT

**Frank Palmer**
Phoenix, Arizona

"I enjoy being able to make garments in the size and color that I want."

102

SKILL LEVEL
Easy

## FINISHED MEASUREMENTS

**Girth Approx:** 22.25 (26.25, 30.25, 34.5, 38.5)"/56.5 (66.5, 77, 87.5, 98)cm
Exact size is determined by placement of hook-and-loop tape closure.
*See Dog Sizes on page 20 for tips on choosing the correct size.*

## MATERIALS

**Approx total:** 200 (240, 288, 346, 414)yd/182 (218, 262, 315, 377)m hemp DK weight yarn

**Color A:** 100 (120, 144, 173, 207)yd/91 (109, 131, 157, 188)m in blue

**Color B:** 100 (120, 144, 173, 207)yd/91 (109, 131, 157, 188)m in green

**Knitting needles**
4.5mm (Size 7 U.S.)
*or size to obtain gauge*

## GAUGE

4.5 sts and 6 rows = 1"/2.5cm in St st

*Always take time to check your gauge.*

# Doggie Saddlebags

Ever feel like Fido gets away with murder while you do all the heavy lifting? Next time you go fishing together, toss this comfy saddlebag jacket on your dog and he can help carry your fishing tackle. The piece is knit as a simple rectangle with stitches picked up for the attached pockets. You measure as you go for a custom fit.

# Instructions

This design consists of a girdle that wraps around the dog's middle, a strap that goes around the dog's chest and attaches to the girdle, and two saddlebags, which are knit onto the girdle. The piece closes at the dog's belly.

## Girdle

With A, cast on 20 (22, 26, 30, 32) sts, work in Garter Stitch for 2 rows. Switch to St st and work for 14 (16, 20, 22, 24) rows.

Work even in Garter St until piece measures 7.75 (9, 10.5, 11.75, 13.25)"/19.5 (23, 26.5, 30, 33.5)cm.

Cont in Garter St, work 2 rows in B. Return to A and work in Garter St until piece measures 15.5 (18, 21, 23.5, 26.5)"/39.5 (44.5, 53.5, 59.5, 67.5)cm from Color B rows.

Cont in Garter St, work 2 rows in B. Return to A and work in Garter St until piece measures 23.25 (27.25, 31.25, 35.5, 39.5)"/59 (69, 79.5, 90, 100.5)cm from cast-on edge, end with a WS row.

Work in St st for 2.25 (2.75, 3.25, 3.5, 4)"/5.5 (7, 8.5, 9, 10)cm, work 2 rows of Garter St. BO all sts.

Fit piece around dog so that two B garter ridges sit an equal distance from the dog's spine on either side of the back.

Pull the piece around the dog's ribcage and check the chest measurement. Safety pin in place so that there is a 2.25 (2.75, 3.25, 3.5, 4)"/5.5 (7, 8.5, 9, 10)cm overlap. This is where the hook-and-loop fastener tape will go.

Measure across the dog's front chest—this will be the length of the strap from left front edge to right front edge of the girdle.

## Strap

With B, pick up 8 sts along left edge of piece, straddling sts so that 4 sts lie on one side of second Color B garter ridge, and 4 sts lay on the other side of garter ridge.

Work in garter st until piece measures 17 (20, 23, 26, 29)"/43 (51, 58.5, 66, 73.5)cm or desired length determined in previous step. BO all sts.

## Left Saddlebag

With B, cast on 20 (22, 26, 30, 32) sts, then continuing on same needle and working just before first contrasting garter ridge, pick up 20 (22, 26, 30, 32) sts across girdle, picking up 1 st for each st on piece—40 (44, 52, 60, 64) sts.

Work in St st for 7.75 (9, 10.5, 11.75, 13.25)"/19.5 (23, 26.5, 30, 33.5)cm, then divide sts equally into bag front and bag back sts—20 (22, 26, 30, 32) sts each side. Turn bag inside out and work a 3-needle bind off across all sts. Repeat for right saddlebag, turning girdle around so that when picking up sts you are working just under contrasting garter ridge row (see illustration on page 105).

### SADDLEBAG FLAPS

Working just above saddlebag, pick up 20 (22, 26, 30, 32) sts across girdle, picking up 1 st for each st on piece—40 (44, 52, 60, 64) sts.

Work in St st for 3"/7.5cm, BO all sts loosely.

## Finishing

Place entire piece in washer and wash on warm, machine dry. Hemp will relax and soften considerably during this process.

Cut piece of loop side of hook-and-loop fastener to fit tip of strap. Hand or machine-sew to underside end of strap. Cut piece of loop fastener to fit across bound off end of girdle. Hand or machine-sew to wrong side (non-saddlebag side) of bound-off edge. Cut pieces of loop fastener to fit underside of saddlebag flap, and sew matching hook fastener to saddlebag front to hold bags closed.

Fit girdle to dog and determine placement of hook-and-loop fastener tape to close girdle. Hand or machine-sew hook-and-loop fastener tape above cast-on edge and just under left pocket.

### This project was knit with

Lana Knits' *All Hemp 6*, 100% hemp, 150yd/137m, 3 1/4oz/91g per skein
(A) 1 (1, 2, 2, 2) skeins, color Deep Sea
(B) 1 (1, 2, 2, 2) skeins, color Sprout

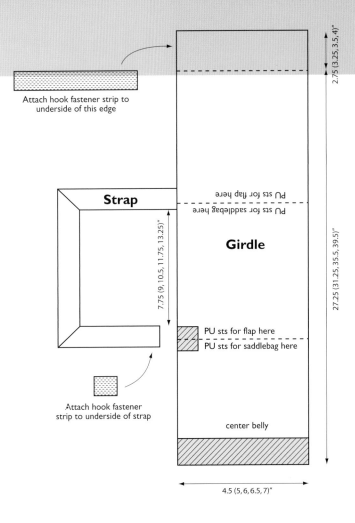

Attach hook fastener strip to underside of this edge

**Strap**

7.75 (9, 10.5, 11.75, 13.25)"

Attach hook fastener strip to underside of strap

2.75 (3.25, 3.5, 4)"

PU sts for flap here
PU sts for saddlebag here

**Girdle**

27.25 (31.25, 35.5, 39.5)"

PU sts for flap here
PU sts for saddlebag here

center belly

4.5 (5, 6, 6.5, 7)"

MEN WHO KNIT

**Ted Myatt**
Ontario, Canada

"I've been knitting for close to 30 years, with a particular interest in lace, and am planning to work some traditional Shetland lace."

SKILL LEVEL
Intermediate

FINISHED
MEASUREMENTS
36 (38, 40, 42, 44, 48, 52,
56)"/91.5 (96.5, 101.5, 106.5,
112, 122, 132, 142)cm
*See Men's Sizes on page
20 for tips on choosing the
correct size.*

MATERIALS
**Approx total:** 4942 (5196,
5364, 5618, 5808, 6252, 6716,
7223)yd/ 4519 (4752, 4905,
5137, 5311, 5717, 6141,
6605)m hemp/wool blend
DK weight yarn

**Color A:** 988 (1039, 1073,
1124, 1162, 1250, 1343,
1445)yd/ 903 (950, 981,
1028, 1063, 1143, 1228,
1321)m in green

**Color B:** 1730 (1819, 1743,
1826, 1742, 1876, 2015,
2167)yd/1582 (1663, 1594,
1670, 1593, 1716, 1843,
1982)m in blue

**Color C:** 1730 (1819, 1743,
1826, 1742, 1876, 2015,
2167)yd/1582 (1663, 1594,
1670, 1593, 1716, 1843,
1982)m in red

**Color D:** 494 (520, 805, 843,
1162, 1250, 1343, 1445)yd/452
(475, 736, 771, 1063, 1143,
1228, 1321)m in gold

# Diagonal Colorblock Pullover

If you've never knit in intarsia before because you thought the technique was difficult or tedious, this sweater will change your mind. Made with large blocks of color, you only change yarns once or twice in a row. The results are stunning, even though the stitch patterns are as easy as pie.

GAUGE

5 sts and 7 rows = 1"/2.5cm
in Chart A patt using 4mm
(Size 6 U.S.) needles

*Always take time to check
your gauge.*

**Knitting needles**

4mm (Size 6 U.S.)
*or size to obtain gauge*

3.75mm (Size 5 U.S.) 16"/41cm
long circular needle

# Instructions

This sweater is knit back and forth in pieces. The location of the color blocks on the back is the reverse of the front. Instructions are given for reversing these colors. If you prefer, work the entire back in a solid color in the patt of your choice.

See page 14 for instructions on intarsia colorwork. When working a stitch in a new color, that st should always be worked in St st, that is:

• When working a RS row, knit this st.

• When working a WS row, purl this st.

## Back

With smaller needles and A, cast on 94 (98, 102, 110, 114, 122, 134, 142) sts. Work in k2, p2 ribbing for 3.25 (3.25, 3.5, 3.5, 3.75, 4, 4, 4.25)"/8.5 (8.5, 9, 9, 9.5, 10, 10, 11)cm.

Change to larger needles and continuing in A, work row 1 of Chart A across all sts.

Cont with A, work in patt as est until piece measures 6.5 (6.25, 6, 5.5, 5.25, 4.5, 4, 3.5)"/16.5 (16, 15, 14, 13.5, 11.5, 10, 9)cm from cast-on edge. End with a RS row.

### ADDING B

**Next row (WS):** Work as est to last 2 sts in row. Change to B and work row 1 of Chart B across these 2 sts.

**Next row (RS):** Work to last B st, then k the next st with B. Cont with A in patt as est to end of row. Be sure to twist yarns at color change to prevent hole.

**Next row (WS):** Work in A as est to 1 st before color change. With B, p1, work rem sts in Chart B as est.

**Rep last 2 rows,** twisting fibers between colors and increasing the B area of piece until work measures 5.75 (5.25, 5, 4.75, 4.5, 4, 3.5, 3)"/14.5 (13.5, 12.5, 12, 11.5, 10, 9, 7.5)cm from cast-on edge. End with a WS row.

## ADDING C

**Next row (RS):** Work as est, cont to work 1 extra st in B and 1 less st in A to last st in row. With C, k 1.

**Next row (WS):** With C p2, with A work in patt as est to 1 st before start of B, with B p1 then work in patt as est to end of row.

**Next row (RS):** With B work in patt as est to first A st, with B k1, work in A as est to 1 st before start of C, with C k3.

Cont with C in Chart C, work 1 st more in C in every row while working 1 st less in A. AT THE SAME TIME continue working 1 st more in B and 1 st less in A on the left side of the piece. The color A area will diminish while the color B and C areas will become larger. Cont until there are no more sts to be worked in A. Work 1 row allowing B and C to meet, then work to start of next WS row. Working with B and C only, work 1 st less in C and 1 st more in B in each row, cont in patt as est, until work measures 3"/7.5cm from end of A. End with a RS row.

## ADDING D

**Next row (WS):** With C, work to 1 st before start of B, with D p2, with B work to end of row, cont in patt as est.

**Next row (RS):** With B, work to 1 st before start of D, with D k4, with C work in patt as est to end of row.

**Next row (WS):** Work to 1 st before start of D. Starting with st 1 of row 1 of chart and working from left to right on chart, work row 1 of Chart D over next 6 sts (end with st 4 of chart). With B work in patt as est to end of row.

**Next row (RS):** With B, work to 1 st before start of D, work in Chart D as est in previous row (being sure to work any st worked in a new color as a St st). Work first C st in D. With C, work in patt as est to end of row.

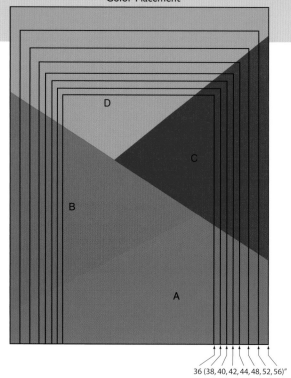

Color Placement

36 (38, 40, 42, 44, 48, 52, 56)"

**Next row (RS):** With C, work to 1 st before start of D. Work in D in patt as est to 1 st past start of B. With B work to end of row in patt as est.

## ARMHOLE SHAPING

Rep last 2 rows until piece measures 14.5 (15, 15, 15.5, 15.75, 16.5, 17.5, 19)"/37 (38, 38, 39.5, 40, 42, 44.5, 48.5)cm from cast-on edge, and work armhole shaping as follows: BO 1 (1, 1, 1, 1, 1, 1, 1) sts at start of every 1 row 8 (8, 8, 10, 10, 12, 12, 14) times—86 (90, 94, 100, 104, 110, 122, 128) sts rem.

Work even until total length of piece measures 21.25 (22.25, 22.25, 23.25, 23.5, 24.75, 26.25, 28.25)"/54 (56.5, 56.5, 59, 59.5, 63, 66.5, 72)cm

## SHOULDER SHAPING

BO 7 (7, 8, 9, 9, 10, 11, 11)sts at start of next 6 rows, then BO 7 (8, 7, 9, 9, 10, 11, 12)sts at start of next 2 rows, then BO rem 30 (32, 32, 32, 32, 34, 34, 38) back neck sts.

# Front

With smaller needles and A, cast on 94 (98, 102, 110, 114, 122, 134, 142) sts.

Work in k2, p2 ribbing for 3.25 (3.25, 3.5, 3.5, 3.75, 4, 4, 4.25)"/8.5 (8.5, 9, 9, 9.5, 10, 10, 11)cm. Change to larger needles and continuing in A, work row 1 of stitch Chart A across all sts. Cont with A, work in patt as est until piece measures 6.5 (6.25, 6, 5.5, 5.25, 4.5, 4, 3.5)"/16.5 (16, 15.5, 14, 13.5, 11.5, 10, 9)cm from cast-on edge. End with a WS row.

## ADDING B

**Next row (RS):** Work as est to last 2 sts in row. Change to B and work row 1 of Chart B across these 2 sts.

**Next row (WS):** Work to last B st, then purl the next st with B. Cont with A in patt as est to end of row. Be sure to twist yarns at color change to prevent hole.

**Next row (RS):** Work in A as est to 1 st before color change. With B, k1, work rem sts in Chart B as est.

**Rep last 2 rows,** twisting fibers between colors and increasing the color B area of piece until work measures 5.75 (5.25, 5, 4.75, 4.5, 4, 3.5, 3)"/14.5 (13.5, 12.5, 12, 11.5, 10, 9, 7.5)cm from cast-on edge. End with a RS row.

## ADDING C

**Next row (WS):** Work as est, cont to work 1 extra st in color B and one less st in color A to last st in row. With C, purl 1.

**Next row (RS):** With C, k2, with A work in patt as est to 1 st before start of B, with B k1, then work in patt as est to end of row.

**Next row (WS):** With B, work in patt as est to first A st, with B p1, work in A as est to 1 st before start of C, with C p3. Cont with C in Chart C, work more st in C in every row while working 1 st less in A. AT THE SAME TIME continue working 1 st more in B and 1 st less in A on the right side of the piece. The color A area will diminish while the color B and C areas will become larger. Continue until there are no more sts to be worked in A. Work 1 row allowing B and C to meet, then work to start of next RS row.

Working with only B and C, work 1 st less in C and 1 st more in B in each row, cont in patt as est, until work measures 3"/7.5cm from end of A. End with a WS row.

## ADDING D

**Next row (RS):** With C, work to 1 st before start of B, with D k2, with B work to end of row, cont in patt as est.

**Next row (WS):** With B, work to 1 st before start of D, with D p4, with C work in patt as est to end of row.

**Next row (RS):** Work to 1 st before start of D. Starting with st 4 of row 1 of chart, work row 1 of Chart D over next 6 sts (end with st 1 of chart). With B, work in patt as est to end of row.

**Next row (WS):** With B, work to 1 st before start of D, work in Chart D as est in previous row (being sure to work any st worked in a new color as a St st). Work first C st in D. With C, work in patt as est to end of row.

**Next row (RS):** With C, work to 1 st before start of D. Work in D in patt as est to 1 st past start of B. With B, work to end of row in patt as est.

## ARMHOLE SHAPING

Rep last 2 rows until piece measures 14.5 (15, 15, 15.5, 15.75, 16.5, 17.5, 19)"/37 (38, 38, 39.5, 40, 42, 44.5, 48.5)cm from cast-on edge, and work armhole shaping as for Back— 86 (90, 94, 100, 104, 110, 122, 128) sts rem.

## NECK SHAPING

When Front measures 20 (20.875, 20.875, 21.75, 22, 23.125, 24.5, 26.375)"/51 (53, 53, 55.5, 56, 58.5, 62, 67)cm from cast-on edge, end with a WS row and work neck shaping as follows:

**Next row (RS):** Work 40 (41, 43, 46, 48, 50, 56, 59) sts, join second ball of yarn, BO center 6 (8, 8, 8, 8, 10, 10, 10) sts, work to end.

Working both sides at the same time, BO 2 (2, 2, 2, 2, 2, 2) sts from each neck edge every row 4 times—32 (33, 35, 38, 40, 42, 48, 51) sts. BO 1 (1, 1, 2, 2, 2, 1, 2) sts from each neck edge every other row 2 times—30 (31, 33, 34, 36, 38, 46, 47) sts. BO 1 (1, 1, 0, 0, 0, 1, 1) st from each neck edge every fourth row 2 times—28 (29, 31, 34, 36, 38, 44, 45) sts rem each shoulder.

AT SAME TIME, when front measures 21.25 (22.25, 22.25, 23.25, 23.5, 24.75, 26.25, 28.25)"/54 (56.5, 56.5, 59, 59.5, 63, 66.5, 72)cm, work shoulder shaping as for back.

# Right Sleeve

With a single strand of C and smaller needles, cast on 36 (38, 38, 38, 38, 40, 42, 42) sts.

Work in k2, p2 ribbing for 3". Change to larger needles and beg with st 1, work row 1 of Chart C across all sts. Cont working in chart as est and AT THE SAME TIME inc 1 st at start of every row 22 (24, 24, 26, 26, 28, 29, 32) times—80 (86, 86, 90, 90, 96, 100, 106) sts. Work even until sleeve measures 16.25 (16.75, 16.75, 17.5, 17.5, 17.75, 18.5, 19)"/41.5 (42.5, 42.5, 44.5, 44.5, 45, 47, 48.5) from end of ribbing. End with a WS row.

## CAP SHAPING

BO 1 st at start of every 1 row 8 (8, 8, 10, 10, 12, 12, 14) times, BO rem 72 (78, 78, 80, 80, 84, 88, 92) sts.

# Left Sleeve

Work as for Right Sleeve using color B and Stitch Chart B for non-ribbing portions of sleeve.

# Turtleneck

Sew shoulder seams.

With smaller circ needles and A, pick up and knit 72 (72, 72, 76, 76, 80, 80, 84) sts around neck opening. Work in k2, p2 ribbing for 6"/15cm (or desired length). BO all sts very loosely with larger needle.

Sew underarm and side seams. Weave in ends.

## This sweater was knit with:

Lana Knits' *Hempwool* DK, 50% hemp/50% wool, 240yd/218m, 3.5oz/100g per skein
(A) 2 (2, 2, 2, 2, 2, 3, 3) skeins, color Sage Green
(B) 3 (3, 3, 3, 3, 4, 4, 4) skeins, color Berry Blue
(C) 3 (3, 3, 3, 3, 4, 4, 4) skeins, color Chili Red
(D) 1 (1, 2, 2, 2, 2, 3, 3) skeins, color Curry

| | K on RS, P on WS |
| | P on RS, K on WS |

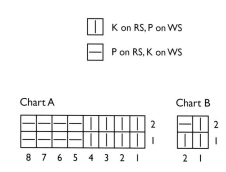

Chart A

8 7 6 5 4 3 2 1

Chart B

2 1

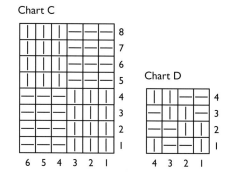

Chart C

6 5 4 3 2 1

Chart D

4 3 2 1

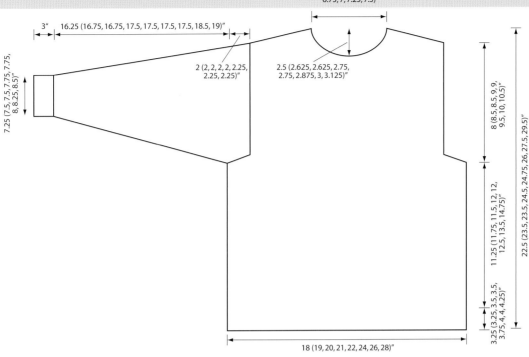

21.25 (21.75, 21.75, 22.5, 23, 23.75, 24.25)"

6.25 (6.5, 6.5, 6.75, 6.75, 7, 7.25, 7.5)"

3"

16.25 (16.75, 16.75, 17.5, 17.5, 17.5, 17.5, 18.5, 19)"

7.25 (7.5, 7.5, 7.75, 7.75, 8, 8.25, 8.5)"

2 (2, 2, 2, 2, 2.25, 2.25, 2.25)"

2.5 (2.625, 2.625, 2.75, 2.75, 2.875, 3, 3.125)"

8 (8.5, 8.5, 9, 9, 9.5, 10, 10.5)"

11.25 (11.75, 11.5, 12, 12, 12.5, 13.5, 14.75)"

22.5 (23.5, 23.5, 24.5, 24.75, 26, 27.5, 29.5)"

3.25 (3.25, 3.5, 3.5, 3.75, 4, 4, 4.25)"

18 (19, 20, 21, 22, 24, 26, 28)"

MEN WHO KNIT

## Doug Iberg
Atlanta, Georgia

"Relying heavily on my established crochet skills, I taught myself to knit with a book and some acrylic yarn."

111

**SKILL LEVEL**
Beginner

**FINISHED MEASUREMENTS**
**Girth:** 8.5 (11.75, 15, 18, 21.25, 24.5, 27.75, 31)"/21.5 (30, 38, 45.5, 54, 62, 70.5, 78.5)cm
*See Dog Sizes on page 20 for tips on choosing the correct size.*

**MATERIALS**
**Approx total:** 630 (630, 630, 945, 945, 945, 1260, 1260)yd/573 (573, 573, 860, 860, 860, 1147, 1147)m wool blend yarn

**Color A:** 300 (300, 300, 450, 450, 450, 600, 600)yd/273 (273, 273, 410, 410, 410, 546, 546)m merino/silk blend DK weight yarn in mauve

**Color B:** 330 (330, 330, 495, 495, 495, 660, 660)yd/300 (300, 300, 450, 450, 450, 601, 601)m wool/cotton blend light worsted weight yarn in multicolor

# Dog Garter Rib Jacket

Made with the same easy stitches as the hat and scarf set on page 115, this jacket is also an excellent beginner project. It's knitted flat and closes with hook-and-loop fastener tape, so the size is adjustable.

## GAUGE

4 sts and 6 rows = 1"/2.5cm in Chart A Garter Rib Patt

*Always take time to check your gauge.*

**Knitting needles**

## 4.5mm (Size 7 U.S.)

*or size to obtain gauge*

4mm (Size 6 U.S.)

1/2"/1.5cm-wide hook-and-loop fastener, 7.75 (10.5, 13.5, 16.5, 19.5, 22.25, 25, 28)"/19.5 (26.5, 34.5, 42, 49.5, 56.5, 63.5, 71)cm long

3.75mm (Size F-5 U.S) crochet hook (optional)

Darning needle for weaving in ends

# Instructions

This sweater is knit back and forth in one piece. An optional single crochet trim is worked around the outside edge for a firm edging.

## Body

With a strand each of A and B held together and larger needle, cast on 19 (25, 31, 37, 45, 51, 57, 63) sts.

**Row 1 (RS):** Beg working Chart A Garter Rib Patt as follows: (k1, p1) rep to end of row, end k1.

**Row 2 (WS):** K all sts.

Cont in st patt as est, inc 3 sts at start of next 2 rows—25 (31, 37, 43, 51, 57, 63, 69) sts.

Inc 1 st at start of every row 10 (18, 24, 30, 36, 42, 50, 56) times, working inc sts into patt—35 (49, 61, 73, 87, 99, 113, 125) sts. If necessary, work even until piece measures 4.5 (6.25, 8, 9.5, 11.25, 13, 14.75, 16.5)"/11.5 (16, 20.5, 24, 28.5, 33, 37.5, 42)cm from cast-on edge. End with a WS row.

### ARMHOLE SHAPING

BO 8 (10, 13, 16, 20, 23, 25, 28) sts from start of next 2 rows, then BO 1 st at start of next 2 (4, 4, 4, 6, 6, 8, 8) rows—17 (25, 31, 37, 41, 47, 55, 61) sts rem.

Work even with no shaping for 0.25 (0, 0.5, 1, 1.125, 1.625, 1.375, 1.875)"/.5 (0, 1.5, 2.5, 3, 4, 3.5, 5)cm.

Inc 1 st at start of next 2 (4, 4, 4, 6, 6, 8, 8) rows, then inc 4 (5, 7, 8, 10, 12, 13, 14)sts at start of next 2 rows—27 (39, 49, 57, 67, 77, 89, 97) sts.

### SHOULDER SHAPING

BO 1 st at start of next 4 (8, 10, 10, 12, 14, 18, 18) rows, then BO 2 (2, 3, 3, 4, 4, 5, 5) sts at start of next 2 rows, then BO 1 (2, 2, 3, 3, 4, 4, 5) sts at start of next 2 rows—17 (23, 29, 35, 41, 47, 53, 59) sts.

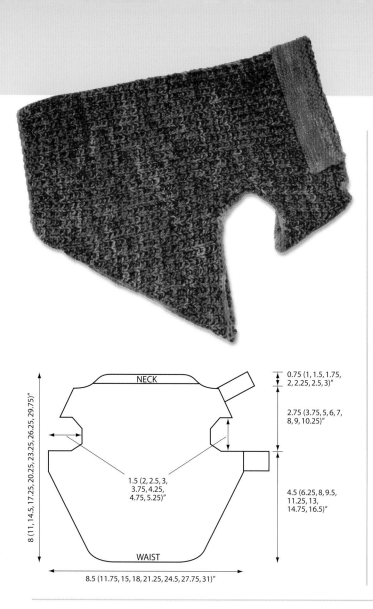

## COLLAR

With a double strand of A and smaller needle, beg working all sts in Garter Stitch.

Inc 1 st each edge every row 5 times, then inc 1 st at start of every row 10 times. Bind off rem sts.

## Finishing

Block piece.

If desired, with a single strand of A, work 1 row of single crochet around edge of garment. Fit garment to dog, determining placement of hook-and-loop fastener when jacket is closed and tabs are pulled across to left side at stomach and front neck. Hand or machine-sew loop side of fastener to garter stitch tabs, and hook side of fastener to garment body.

### This sweater was knit with:

(A) 2 (2, 2, 3, 3, 3, 4, 4) hanks of Lorna's Laces' *Swirl DK*, 85% merino/15% silk, 150yd/137m, 1.75oz/50g per hank, color 2ns Manzanita
(B) 2 (2, 2, 3, 3, 3, 4, 4) hanks of Lorna's Laces' *Dove*, 80% wool/20% cotton, 165yd/150m, 2oz/56g per hank, color 74 Motherlode

Diagram labels:
NECK
WAIST
0.75 (1, 1.5, 1.75, 2, 2.25, 2.5, 3)"
2.75 (3.75, 5, 6, 7, 8, 9, 10.25)"
1.5 (2, 2.5, 3, 3.75, 4.25, 4.75, 5.25)"
4.5 (6.25, 8, 9.5, 11.25, 13, 14.75, 16.5)"
8 (11, 14.5, 17.25, 20.25, 23.25, 26.25, 29.75)"
8.5 (11.75, 15, 18, 21.25, 24.5, 27.75, 31)"

MEN WHO KNIT

## Jason Weisman
Maryland

"Knitting helps me to be calm and focused— and it's a good conversation starter with girls."

*Jason, a 15-year old knitter with Asperger's Syndrome, is a sophomore in high school.*

**FINISHED
MEASUREMENTS**
**Hat to fit head
circumference:** 18 (19.5,
21, 22.5, 24)"/45.5 (49.5,
53.5, 57, 61)cm
**Scarf:** 8 1/2"/21.5cm wide
by desired length

# Garter Rib
# Scarf and Hat

This easy hat and scarf set is a great project for the new
knitter, and the perfect gift for yourself or your best friend.

**MATERIALS**
**Approx total:** 1260yd/1147m
of wool blend DK and light
worsted weight yarn

**Color A:** 450yd/410m
merino/silk blend DK weight
yarn in mauve

**Color B:** 495yd/450m
wool/cotton blend light worsted
weight yarn in multicolor

**Color C:** 150yd/137m
merino/silk blend DK weight
yarn in variegated grays

**Color D:** 165yd/150m
wool/cotton blend light
worsted weight yarn in
variegated grays

**Knitting needles**
4.5mm (Size 7 U.S.) circular
needle 16"/40.5cm long and
double-pointed needles *or
size to obtain gauge*

5 stitch markers
(1 in a contrasting color)

Darning needle for
weaving in ends

**GAUGE**
4 sts and 6 rows = 1" in
Chart A Garter Rib Patt

*Always take time to check
your gauge.*

# Instructions

## Hat

With a strand each of C and D held together, cast on 72 (80, 84 ,92, 96) sts, join to work in the round. ALL COLOR CHANGES K AS IS.

Work in k2, p2 ribbing for 8 rows. Change to a strand each of A and B held together, cont in ribbing patt until piece measures 2.5 (2.75, 3 ,3.25, 3.5)"/6.5 (7, 7.5, 8.5, 9)cm.

In last round of ribbing dec 0 (2, 0, 2, 0) sts evenly around— 72 (78, 84, 90, 96) sts.

**Next round:** Knit all sts, placing a marker every 12 (13, 14, 15, 16) sts, creating 6 equal sections. Use a contrasting marker at start of round.

Work in Chart A Garter Rib Patt for a total of 12 (14, 16 ,18, 20) rows from end of k2, p2 ribbing.

### CROWN DECREASES

**Rounds 1 and 3:** (K1, p1) around.

**Round 2:** (K to 2 sts before next marker, k2tog-LS) rep around—66 (72, 78, 84, 90) sts

**Round 4:** (K2tog-RS, k to next marker) rep around—60 (66, 72, 78, 84) sts.

**Rounds 5 and 7:** (P1, k1) rep around.

**Round 6:** (K to 2 sts before next marker, k2tog-LS) rep to end of round—54 (60, 66, 72, 78) sts.

**Round 8:** (K2tog-RS, k to next marker) rep to end of round— 48 (54, 60, 66, 72) sts.

Rep last 8 rounds until only 6 sts rem, changing to dpns when sts no longer fit on circ. Break yarn, leaving a 7"/18cm tail. With darning needle, draw tail through rem sts. Weave in ends

## Scarf

With a strand each of C and D held together and smaller needles, cast on 34 sts.

Work in k2, p2 ribbing for 8 rows, knitting the first and last 2 sts of each row to create a Garter St edge.

Change to a strand of each A and B held together, cont in patt as est for 8 more rows.

Work in Chart A Garter Rib Patt until scarf is desired length. (A man's muffler generally measures from the tip of the head to the waist. A man's scarf generally measures from the tip of the head to the ground.)

Work in k2, p2 ribbing for 8 rows, knitting the first and last 2 sts of each row to create a Garter Stitch edge. Change to a strand of C and D held together and cont in patts as est for 8 more rows.

BO all sts loosely in rib. Weave in ends.

### This hat and scarf were knit with:

(A) 3 hanks of Lorna's Laces' *Swirl DK*, 85% merino/15% silk, 150yd/137m, 1.75oz/50g per hank, color 2ns Manzanita
(B) 3 hanks of Lorna's Laces' *Dove*, 80% wool/20% cotton, 165yd/150m, 2oz/56g per hank, color 74 Motherlode
(C) 1 hank of Lorna's Laces' *Swirl DK*, 85% merino/15% silk, 150yd/137m, 1.75oz/50g per hank, color 102 Mineshaft
(D) 1 hank of Lorna's Laces' *Dove*, 80% wool/20% cotton, 165yd/150m, 2oz/56g per hank, color 102 Mineshaft

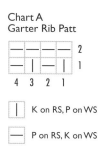

**Chart A**
**Garter Rib Patt**

```
|— — —|        2
|— | —|        1
 4 3 2 1
```

| K on RS, P on WS

— P on RS, K on WS

| Back and Forth: | In the Round: |
|---|---|
| Row 1: (K1, P1) across | Rnd 1: (K1, P1) around |
| Row 2: Knit | Rnd 2: Purl |

**FINISHED MEASUREMENTS**
**Chest:** 38 (42, 46, 50, 54, 58, 64, 68)"/96.5 (106.5, 117, 127, 137, 147.5, 162.5, 172.5)cm
*See Men's Sizes on page 20 for tips on choosing the correct size.*

**MATERIALS**
**Approx total:** 1195 (1270, 1345, 1420, 1495, 1644, 1793, 1942)yd/1087 (1156, 1224, 1292, 1360, 1496, 1632, 1767)m of wool DK weight yarn

**Color A:** 996 (1058, 1121, 1183, 1246, 1370, 1494, 1618)yd/906 (963, 1020, 1077, 1134, 1247, 1360, 1472)m in variegated light greens and blues

**Color B:** 199 (212, 224, 237, 249, 274, 299, 324)yd/181 (193, 204, 216, 227, 249, 272, 295)m in solid green

**Knitting needles**
4.5mm (Size 7 U.S.)

Darning needle for sewing seams and weaving in ends

**GAUGE**
5.5 sts and 6.25 rows = 1"/2.5cm in St st

*Always take time to check your gauge.*

# Double Roll-Neck Simple Sweater

Variegated yarn and the easy rolled neck and cuffs provide this sweater with flair without making it difficult to knit. To frame the sweater, the second layer on the neckline and cuffs can be knit in a solid color.

# Instructions

This sweater is knit back and forth in pieces. The instructions include a "Neck Shaping Translation for New Knitters" to make this truly easy for the beginning knitter.

## Back

Cast on 104 (116, 126, 138, 148, 160, 176, 188) sts. Work in St st for 24.5 (25.5, 25.25, 26.25, 26.25, 27.25, 28.75, 30.5) " 62 (65, 64, 66.5, 66.5, 69, 73, 77.5)cm. Bind off all sts.

## Front

Cast on 104 (116, 126, 138, 148, 160, 176, 188) sts. Work in St st for 21.25 (22.125, 21.875, 22.75, 22.75, 23.625, 25, 26.625)"/54 (56, 55.5, 58, 58, 60, 63.5, 67.5)cm. End with a WS row.

### NECK SHAPING

**Note:** See Neck Shaping Translation for New Knitters below for line-by-line instructions.

**Next row (RS):** K 49 (54, 58, 64, 69, 75, 82, 88) sts, join 2nd ball of yarn and BO center 6 (8, 10, 10, 10, 10, 12, 12) sts, then knit rem 49 (54, 58, 64, 69, 75, 82, 88) sts. BO 2 sts at neck edge every row 4 times, then BO 1 (2, 1, 1, 1, 2, 1, 1) at neck edge every other row 4 times, then BO 1 st at neck edge every fourth row twice—35 (36, 44, 50, 55, 57, 68, 74) sts rem each shoulder. Work until front measures same as back, BO rem shoulder sts.

### Neck Shaping Translation for New Knitters

**Next row (RS):** K49 (54, 58, 64, 69, 75, 82, 88) sts—this will be the right shoulder. Join 2nd ball of yarn and BO center 6 (8, 10, 10, 10, 10, 12, 12) sts. Continuing with 2nd ball of yarn, k 49 (54, 58, 64, 69, 75, 82, 88) rem sts—this will be the left shoulder. Turn work.

**Next row (WS):** P to 3 sts before neck BO, p3tog. Leave yarn and move over to right shoulder and with the right shoulder ball of yarn BO 2 sts, then p to end of row (this is what's known as working both shoulders on the same needle at the same time).

Next row (RS): K to 3 sts before neck BO, k3tog. Leave yarn and move over to left shoulder and with the left shoulder ball of yarn BO 2 sts, then knit to end of row.

**Repeat the last 2 rows** one more time—41 (46, 50, 56, 61, 67, 74, 80) sts rem.

**Next row (WS);** P all sts on both shoulders with no decreasing or binding off.

**Next row (RS):** K all sts on right shoulder with no decreasing. Move to left shoulder and BO 1 (2, 1, 1, 1, 2, 1, 1) sts, then work to end of row.

**Next row (WS):** P all sts on left shoulder with no decreasing, then move to right shoulder and BO 1 (2, 1, 1, 1, 2, 1, 1) sts, then work to end of row.

**Rep the last 2 rows** 3 more times—37 (38, 46, 52, 57, 59, 70, 76) sts rem.

**Next row (RS):** K all sts on right shoulder with no decreasing, move to left shoulder and BO 1 st, then work to end of row.

**Next row (WS):** P all sts on left shoulder with no decreasing, then move to right shoulder and BO 1 st, then work to end of row.

**Work 2 rows** even with no decreasing.

**Repeat the last 4 rows** once more—35 (36, 44, 50, 55, 57, 68, 74) sts rem each shoulder. Work until front measures same as back, BO rem shoulder sts.

## Sleeves (make 2)

CO 46 (48, 48, 50, 50, 50, 52, 54) sts. Work in St st with no inc for 4 rows, then k 2 rows to create a garter ridge. Beg inc 1 st each edge every 4 (4, 4, 2, 2, 2, 2, 2) rows 33 (35, 35, 37, 37, 40, 41, 43) times—112 (118, 118, 124, 124, 130, 134, 140) sts.

Work even until sleeve measures 19.25 (19.75, 19.75, 20.25, 20.25, 20.75, 21.5, 22)"/49 (50, 50, 51.5, 51.5, 52.5, 54.5, 56)cm. Bind off all sts.

## Finishing

Block all pieces. Sew shoulder seams.

### ROLL NECKLINE

With a single strand of A, pick up and knit 100 (104, 104, 104, 104, 108, 112, 112) sts around neck opening, join. K 1 round, p 1 round, k 6 rounds. Bind off loosely.

### CONTRASTING ROLL NECKLINE

Turn sweater inside out. With a single strand of B and working on the wrong side of the neck opening, pick up and knit 100 (104, 104, 104, 104, 108, 112, 112) sts at Rev St st ridge by inserting needle into "smile" part of purl stitch (each purl stitch has a "smile" and a "frown"). Join to work in the round, then turn so you are working on the RS.

Next round (RS): K all sts. Continue in St st for 8 rounds, bind off all sts loosely.

### CONTRASTING CUFFS

With B and working on the wrong side of wrist, pick up and knit 46 (48, 48, 50, 50, 50, 52, 54) sts in the same manner as you picked up sts at neck opening. Turn. Work in St st for 8 rows. BO loosely.

Sew in sleeves. Sew underarm and side seams, sewing contrasting inner cuff separately.

Weave in ends. Block.

**This sweater was knit with:**

Art Yarns' *Ultramerino* 6, 100% merino wool, 274yd/249m, 3.5 oz/100g per skein

(A) 4 (4, 4, 4, 5, 5, 5, 6) skeins, color UM104 Light Greens/Blue

(B) 1 (1, 1, 1, 1, 1, 2, 2) skeins, color UM216 Light Leaf Green

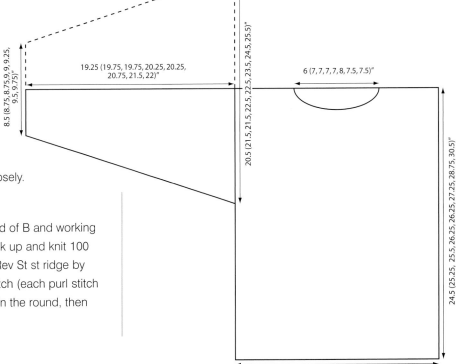

8.5 (8.75, 8.75, 9, 9, 9.25, 9.5, 9.75)"

19.25 (19.75, 19.75, 20.25, 20.25, 20.75, 21.5, 22)"

20.5 (21.5, 21.5, 22.5, 22.5, 23.5, 24.5, 25.5)"

6 (7, 7, 7, 7, 8, 7.5, 7.5)"

24.5 (25.25, 25.5, 26.25, 26.25, 27.25, 28.75, 30.5)"

19 (21, 23, 25, 27, 29, 32, 34)"

SKILL LEVEL
Easy

FINISHED
MEASUREMENTS
**Girth:** 9.5 (12.5, 15.5, 18.5, 21.5, 25.5, 28.5, 31.5)"/24 (32, 39.5, 47, 54.5, 65, 72.5, 80)cm
*See Dog Sizes on page 20 for tips on choosing the correct size.*

# Double Roll-Neck Doggie Jacket

A simple yarn over increase adds a lacy texture to this easy jacket. The ties are added after the knitting is complete, giving the jacket a flexible fit.

## MATERIALS

**Approx total:** 548 (548, 548, 822, 822, 1096, 1096, 1096)yd/499 (499, 499, 748, 748, 997, 997, 997)m of wool DK weight yarn

**Color A:** 274 (274, 274, 548, 548, 822, 822, 822)yd/249 (249, 249, 499, 499, 748, 748, 748)m in variegated light greens and blues

**Color B:** 274yd/249m in solid green

**Knitting needles**
4.5mm (Size 7 U.S.) straight and double-pointed needles *or size to obtain gauge*

4mm (Size 6 U.S.) straight and double-pointed needles

4mm (Size G-6 U.S.) crochet hook

8 stitch markers (1 in a contrasting color)

Darning needle for sewing seams and weaving in ends

## GAUGE
4 sts and 6 rows = 1" using 4.5mm (Size 7 U.S.) needles

*Always take time to check your gauge.*

# Instructions
Sweater is worked back and forth in one piece.

## Body
With larger needle and A, cast on 20 (28, 36, 44, 44, 52, 60, 68) sts. Knit 2 rows.

**BEG SHAPING**
**Row 1 (RS):** K10 (14, 18, 22, 22, 26, 30, 34) sts, place marker (pm), YO, k to end.

**Row 2 (WS):** K10 (14, 18, 22, 22, 26, 30, 34) sts, pm, YO, k to end.

**Row 3 (RS):** K2, (p2, k2) rep to marker, sm, YO, k to next marker, sm, (k2, p2) rep to last 2 sts, end k2.

**Row 4 (WS):** K2, work in ribbing as est to marker, sm, YO, p to next marker, sm, work in ribbing as est to last 2 sts, end k2.

**Rep rows 3 and 4** until there are 38 (50, 62, 74, 86, 102, 114, 126) sts total.

**Next row:** Work in ribbing as est to marker, sm, YO, k2tog-LS, k to next marker, sm, work as est to last 2 sts, k2.

**Next row:** K2, work in ribbing as est to marker, sm, YO, p2tog, p to next marker, sm, work as est to last 2 sts, k2.

**Rep last 2 rows** until piece measures 4.75 (6.5, 8.25, 10.25, 12, 13.75, 15.5, 17.25)"/12 (16.5, 21, 26, 30.5, 35, 39.5, 44)cm from cast on edge. End with a WS row.

## ARMHOLE DECREASE

BO 7 (9, 10, 14, 16, 19, 21, 23) sts from start of next 2 rows, then dec 1 st at start of next 2 (2, 4, 4, 4, 6, 6, 6) rows—22 (30, 38, 42, 50, 58, 66, 74) sts rem.

**Next row:** Work in ribbing as est to marker, sm, YO, k2tog-LS, k to next marker, sm, work as est to last 2 sts, k2.

**Next row:** K2, work in ribbing as est to marker, sm, YO, p2tog, p to next marker, sm, work as est to last 2 sts, k2.

**Rep last 2 rows** 2 (2, 3, 3, 3, 4, 4, 4) times. End with a WS row.

## ARMHOLE INCREASE

Cont in patt as est, inc 1 st at start of next 2 (2, 4, 4, 4, 6, 6, 6) rows, then cast on 4 (5, 5, 7, 8, 10, 11, 12) sts at start of next 2 rows, working new sts into k2, p2 ribbing—32 (42, 52, 60, 70, 84, 94, 104) sts.

## SHOULDER SHAPING

**Next row (RS):** Cont in patt as est, work to marker, sm, YO, k3tog-LS, k to marker, sm, work in ribbing as est to last 2 sts, end k2.

**Next row (WS):** K2, work in ribbing as est to marker, sm, YO, p3tog, p to marker, sm, work in ribbing as est to last 2 sts, end k2.

**Rep last 2 rows** 5 (6, 7, 7, 8, 11, 12, 13) times—22 (30, 38, 46, 54, 62, 70, 78) sts, then BO 1 (1, 2, 2, 3, 3, 4, 4) sts at start of next 2 rows, then BO 1 (1, 2, 2, 3, 3, 4, 4) sts at start of next 2 rows—18 (26, 30, 38, 42, 50, 54, 62) sts.

## Collar

With smaller needles, knit 2 rows, then work 12 rows in St st. BO very loosely.

With B and smaller needles, pick up and knit 1 st into each st in purl st on wrong side at start of 12 collar rows. Work in St st for 16 rows so that the B layer curls under the A layer.

## Finishing

Block piece. With B, work 1 row of single crochet around edge of garment.

Fit garment to dog, determining length of I-cord ties when jacket is closed at stomach and front neck. With dpns and B, make 4 pieces of I-cord (see page 17) to match these measurements, and stitch to dog jacket at point where B collar roll begins and at widest point of jacket (before armhole shaping).

Fit jacket onto dog and tie I-cord so that it fits snugly. Due to the elastic nature of knit fabric, it may not be necessary to retie the jacket each time the dog wears it.

Weave in ends.

**This jacket was knit with:**

Art Yarns' *Ultramerino 6*, 100% merino wool, 274yd/250m, 3.5 oz/100g per skein
(A) 1 (1, 1, 2, 2, 3, 3, 3) skeins, color UM104 Light Greens/Blue
(B) 1 skein, color UM216 Light Leaf Green

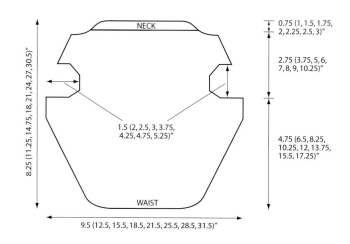

SKILL LEVEL
Intermediate

FINISHED
MEASUREMENTS
**Chest:** 36 (40, 42, 44, 46, 50,
54, 58)"/91.5 (101.5, 106.5,
112, 117, 127, 137, 147.5)cm
*See Men's Sizes on page
20 for tips on choosing the
correct size.*

MATERIALS
**Approx total:** 756 (779,
803, 828, 854, 880, 960,
1040)yd/688 (709, 731,
753, 777, 801, 874, 946)m
wool/silk/cashmere blend Aran
weight yarn in dark gray

**Knitting needles**
5mm (Size 8 U.S.) circular
needle at least 24"/61cm long
*or size to obtain gauge*

4mm (Size 6 U.S.) circular
needle at least 24"/61cm long

Cable needle
(optional, see page 16)

Five ¾"/2cm buttons

Sewing needle and
thread to match yarn
for sewing on buttons

Darning needle for sewing
seams and weaving in ends

GAUGE
4 sts and 6 rows = 1"/2.5cm
in St st using 5mm (Size 8
U.S.) needles

*Always take time to check
your gauge.*

# Gray Cabled Vest

This vest is knit in the traditional Aran weight yarn used
in Ireland to knit classic cabled sweaters. The patterns
on the left and right fronts are mirror images, but both
charts are provided so you don't have to reverse the
cable crossings in your head.

# Instructions

Body is worked in one piece to armholes. Then fronts and back are worked separately to shoulders. The cable sections draw in like ribbing, making the body smaller than you might assume from your St st gauge swatch.

## Body

With A, cast on 153 (173, 183, 193, 203, 223, 243, 253) sts.

**Next row (RS):** (K3, p2), rep to last 3 sts, k3. Cont in k3, p2 ribbing for 6 rows, end with a WS row, decreasing 1 st in middle of last row—152 (172, 182, 192, 202, 222, 242, 252) sts rem.

**Next row (RS):** K3, p2, work Right Front Cable Chart A across next 28 sts, p24 (34, 39, 44, 49, 59, 69, 74) sts, work Back Cable Chart B across next 38 sts, p24 (34, 39, 44, 49, 59, 69, 74) sts, work Left Front Cable Chart C across next 28 sts, p2, k3.

Cont in charted cable patts as est until body measures 10 (11.25, 11.75, 12.5, 13, 14.25, 15.5, 16.5)"/25.5 (28.5, 30, 32, 33, 36, 39.5, 42)cm from cast-on edge, or desired body length. End with a WS row.

## Armhole Shaping

**Next row (RS):** Cont in charted patt as est, work 30 (34, 36, 38, 40, 44, 48, 50) right front sts, BO 16 (18, 18, 20, 20, 22, 24, 26) sts for right armhole, work 60 (68, 74, 76, 82, 90, 98, 100) back sts, BO 16 (18, 18, 20, 20, 22, 24, 26) sts for left armhole, work rem 30 (34, 36, 38, 40, 44, 48, 50) left front sts.

## Back

Cont working on center 60 (68, 74, 76, 82, 90, 98, 100) back sts with no shaping until armhole depth measures 9.5 (9.75, 10, 10, 9.75, 10.25, 10.5, 11)"/24 (25, 25.5, 25.5, 25, 26, 26.5, 28)cm.

### SHOULDER SHAPING

BO 4 (6, 6, 6, 8, 8, 10, 10) sts at start of next 4 rows, then BO 6 (6, 8, 8, 6, 10, 8, 8) sts at start of next 2 rows. BO rem 32 (32, 34, 36, 38, 38, 42, 44) sts.

## Fronts

Work fronts both at the same time or separately, as desired. Working on 30 (34, 36, 38, 40, 44, 48, 50) sts for each front, work even until armhole depth measures 7 (7.125, 7.375, 7.25, 7, 7.375, 7.5, 7.875)"/17.5 (18, 18.5, 18.5, 17.5, 18.5, 19, 20)cm.

### NECK SHAPING

BO 4 (4, 5, 6, 7, 7, 9, 8) sts at neck edge at start of next row, then BO 2 (2, 2, 2, 2, 2, 2, 2) at neck edge every row 3 times, then BO 2 (2, 2, 2, 2, 2, 2, 2) at neck edge every other row 2 times, then BO 1 (1, 1, 1, 1, 1, 1, 2) at neck edge every other row 2 times—14 (18, 19, 20, 21, 25, 27, 28) sts rem.

AT SAME TIME, when piece measures 8.5 (8.75, 9, 9, 8.75, 9.25, 9.5, 10)"/21.5 (22, 23, 23, 22, 23.5, 24, 25.5)cm from start of armhole shaping, work shoulder shaping as for back.

## Front Edgings

With smaller needle, pick up and knit 81 (87, 91, 93, 95, 102, 108, 114) sts along right front edge, place marker (pm), pick up and knit 1 st at corner, pm, pick up and knit 61 (63, 63, 67, 67, 69, 73, 79) sts around neck opening, pm, pick up and knit 1 st at corner, pm, pick up and knit 81 (87, 91, 93, 95, 102, 108, 114) sts down left front edge—225 (239, 247, 255, 259, 275, 291, 309) sts.

**Next row (WS):** (K to st between corner markers, k3 sts into this st), rep once, k to end.

### BUTTONHOLE ROW

**Next row (RS):** (K to middle st between markers, k3 sts into this corner st), rep once, k 7 (8, 8, 5, 7, 10, 7, 8), (BO next 5 sts, k11 [12, 13, 14, 14, 15, 17, 18]), rep across, ending with k10 (11, 11, 12, 12, 12, 13, 14).

C3/1 - Slip 3 sts, p1, k3 slipped sts in front of p st.

C1/3 - Slip 1 st. k3, p1 slipped st in back of 3 sts.

C1/3 R - Slip 3 sts. k3. k3 slipped sts in back of 3 k sts.

C3/3 L - Slip 3 sts. k3. k3 slipped sts in front of 3 k sts.

Work rows in box twice

**Next row (WS):** (K to first bound off st, cable cast on 5 sts) rep to marker, (k to center st between corner markers, k3 sts into this st), rep once, k to end.

**Next row (RS):** (K to middle st between markers, k3 sts into this corner st), rep once, k to end.

Rep last row until 10 rows of Garter St have been worked in total. Bind off rem 241 (255, 263, 271, 275, 291, 307, 325) sts loosely.

## Armhole Facing

With smaller needle, pick up and knit 16 (18, 18, 20, 20, 22, 24, 26) sts along bottom edge of armhole, pm, pick up and knit 43 (44, 45, 45, 44, 46, 47, 50) sts along side edge of armhole to shoulder, pick up and knit 43 (44, 45, 45, 44, 46, 47, 50) sts down armhole to start of round, pm—104 (108, 110, 112, 110, 116, 120, 128) sts.

**Next round:** K2tog-RS, k to 2 sts before marker, k2tog-LS, sm, k2tog-RS, k to 2 sts before marker, k2tog-LS—100 (104, 106, 108, 106, 112, 116, 124) sts rem.

**Next round:** Purl all sts, slipping markers with no decreasing.

**Rep last 2 rounds** three more times until 88 (92, 94, 96, 94, 100, 104, 112) sts rem. BO all sts loosely.

## Finishing

Weave in ends. Block to measurements. Cables are like ribbing, they can draw in a lot or be blocked out loosely. Do not press the cables or the pattern will be flattened.

**This vest was knit with:**

7 (7, 8, 8, 8, 8, 9, 10) skeins of Queensland Collection's *Khatmandu Aran*, 85% Merino Wool, 10% Silk, 5% cashmere, 104yd/95m, 1.75oz/50g per skein, color 118 Dark Gray

Chart B
Back

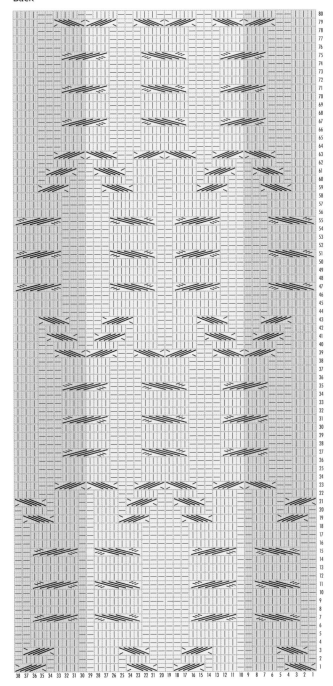

Chart A
Right Front

Chart C
Left Front

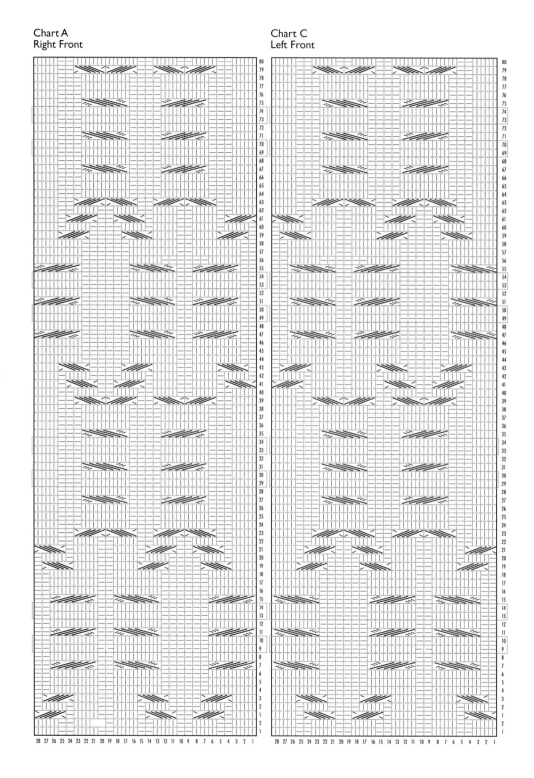

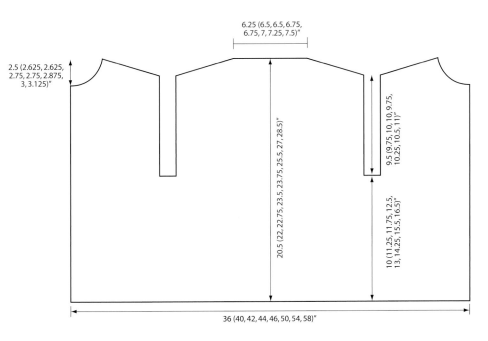

6.25 (6.5, 6.5, 6.75, 6.75, 7, 7.25, 7.5)"

2.5 (2.625, 2.625, 2.75, 2.75, 2.875, 3, 3.125)"

20.5 (22, 22.75, 23.5, 23.75, 25.5, 27, 28.5)"

9.5 (9.75, 10, 10, 9.75, 10.25, 10.5, 11)"

10 (11.25, 11.75, 12.5, 13, 14.25, 15.5, 16.5)"

36 (40, 42, 44, 46, 50, 54, 58)"

## Mark Newport
Mesa, Arizona

"Having my full-body, hand knit, super hero costumes exhibited at the Arizona State University Art Museum, and receiving a grant from the Creative Capital Foundation to make prints centering around my costumes have been two highlights for me in the past year."

*Mark Newport is a well-known fiber and installation artist whose work includes many hand-knit pieces.*

## SKILL LEVEL
Easy

## FINISHED MEASUREMENTS
**Girth:** 8.5 (11.75, 15, 18, 21.25, 24.5, 27.75, 31)"/21.5 (30, 38, 45.5, 54, 62, 70.5, 78.5)cm
*See Dog Sizes on page 20 for tips on choosing the correct size.*

## MATERIALS
**Approx total:** 88 (104, 120, 138, 159, 180, 210, 241)yd/80 (95, 109, 126, 145, 164, 191, 219)m wool/silk/cashmere blend Aran weight yarn in dark gray

**Knitting needles**
5mm (Size 8 U.S.)
*or size to obtain gauge*

4mm (Size 6 U.S.)

Cable needle
(optional, see page 16)

1/2"/1.5cm wide hook-and-loop fastener, 6"/15cm long

## GAUGE
4 sts and 6 rows = 1"/2.5cm in St st using 5mm (Size 8 U.S.) needles

*Always take time to check your gauge.*

# Gray Cabled Dog Vest

Made to coordinate with the cabled vest on page 123, this dog sweater features a much simpler cable pattern. If you've never knitted cables before, try this before working on a more complicated cable project.

## Instructions
Sweater is worked back and forth in one piece.

## Body
With larger needles, cast on 18 (26, 34, 38, 46, 50, 58, 66) sts.

**Row 1 (RS):** K2, place marker (pm), (p2, k2) rep to last 2 sts, pm, k2.

**Next row:** K2, slip marker (sm), M1, work in ribbing as est to marker, sm, k2.

**Rep last row** until there are 34 (50, 66, 74, 90, 98, 114, 130) sts, end with a WS row.

**Next row (RS):** K2, sm, (k6, p2) rep to end of row, end k2.

**Next row (WS):** K2, sm, (p6, k2) rep to end of row, end k2.

**Next row (RS):** K2, (work row 1 of Chart A Cable Patt over next 6 sts, p2) rep to end of row, end k2.

**Next row (WS):** Work in charted patt as est. Cont in cable patt as est, work even until piece measures 4.75 (6.5, 8.25, 10.25, 12, 13.75, 15.5, 17.25)"/12 (16.5, 21, 26, 30.5, 35, 39.5, 44)cm from cast-on edge. End with a WS row.

### ARMHOLE SHAPING DECREASE

BO 4 (8, 10, 10, 14, 16, 16, 20) rows from start of next 2 rows—26 (34, 46, 54, 62, 66, 82, 90) sts.

Work even with no shaping in cable patt as est, working outer 2 sts on either edge in Garter St (knit the first 2 and last 2 sts of every row), until armhole depth measures 0.75 (1.25, 1.5, 1.75, 2.25, 2.5, 2.75, 3.25)"/2 (3, 4, 4.5, 5.5, 6.5, 7, 8.5)cm.

**Note:** If there are fewer than 8 sts in a cable panel, work those sts in St st.

### ARMHOLE SHAPING INCREASE

Inc 1 st at start of next 2 (2, 2, 2, 4, 4, 4, 6) rows, then cast on 2 (4, 5, 5, 6, 7, 7, 9) sts at start of next 2 rows—32 (44, 58, 66, 78, 84, 100, 114) sts, working new sts into cable patt as est.

### SHOULDER SHAPING

Cont in cable patt, BO 1 st at start of next 10 (14, 20, 20, 24, 22, 30, 36) rows—22 (30, 38, 46, 54, 62, 70, 78) sts.

BO 1 (1, 2, 2, 3, 3, 4, 4) sts at start of next 4 rows—18 (26, 30, 38, 42, 50, 54, 62) sts.

## Collar

Switch to smaller needles and work k2, p2 ribbing as follows:

Working first 2 and last 2 sts from each cable panel as K sts, and other sts in ribbing as est.

Work in Ribbing for 0.75 (1.25, 1.5, 1.75, 2.25, 2.5, 2.75, 3.25)"/2 (3, 4, 4.5, 5.5, 6.5, 7, 8.5)cm. BO all sts loosely in ribbing.

## Neck Strap

With smaller needle, pick up 9 (13, 15, 15, 19, 21, 21, 25) sts along right shoulder edge (see schematic) and work in Garter Stitch for 1.5 (2.25, 2.75, 3.5, 4, 4.5, 5.25, 5.75)"/4 (5.5, 7, 9, 10, 11.5, 13.5, 14.5)cm.

Work 4 rows in St st. BO all sts loosely.

## Belly Strap

Repeat Neck Strap instructions along right edge just below armhole to create belly strap.

## Finishing

Weave in ends. Try garment on dog to check length of belly and neck straps. Sew hook portion of hook-and-loop fastener to underside of left edge corresponding to points where sts were picked up on right edge. Sew loop portion of hook-and-loop fastener to right side of the ends of the neck and belly strap.

Block to measurements. Cables are like ribbing, they can draw in a lot or be blocked out loosely. Do not press the cables or the pattern will be flattened.

### This vest was knit with:

1 (1, 2, 2, 2, 2, 3, 3) skeins of Queensland Collection's *Khatmandu Aran*, 85% merino wool, 10% silk, 5% cashmere, 104yd/95m, 1.75oz/50g per skein, color 118 Dark Gray

**Chart A**

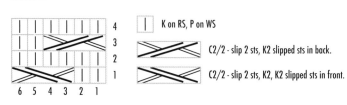

| | K on RS, P on WS |
| | C2/2 - slip 2 sts, K2 slipped sts in back. |
| | C2/2 - slip 2 sts, K2, K2 slipped sts in front. |

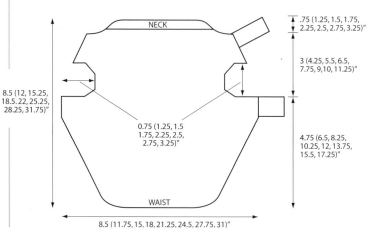

130

**SKILL LEVEL**
Easy

**FINISHED
MEASUREMENTS**
**Circumference:** 20 (21.5,
23)"/51 (54.5, 58.5)cm

**MATERIALS**
**Approx total:** 550yd/500m
silk bulky weight yarn

**Color A:** 220yd/200m in red

**Color B:** 220yd/200m in black

**Color C:** 110yd/100m in white

**Knitting needles**
6mm (Size 10 U.S.) circular
needle 12"/30.5cm long
and double-pointed needles
*or size to obtain gauge*

5mm (Size 8 U.S.) 24" circular
needle 12"/30.5cm long and
double-pointed needles

1 stitch marker

Darning needle for
weaving in ends

**GAUGE**
3.25 sts and 4 rows =
1"/2.5cm in St st using 6mm
(Size 10 U.S.) needles

*Always take time to check
your gauge.*

# Man's Dreadlock Hat

This ribbed hat is covered in knitted dreadlocks. It's quite
easy to make, comfortable to wear, and will without fail,
bring a smile to the face of the beholder. The dreadlocks
are made with a finger knitting technique the author
invented just for this purpose.

## Special Stitch
### MAKE DREADLOCK (MD)
Knit into next stitch, but do not slide stitch off of the left-hand needle. With your right index finger pull the new loop off of the right-hand needle and pull loop toward you, making total length of loop twice the length from needle to your right hand as desired for finished dreadlock.

Twist loop clockwise until it is very, very tight, then slip loop off of right index finger onto the left-hand needle, allowing loop to twist onto itself. Knit loop together with stitch from which it is drawn to lock dreadlock in place.

If necessary, use your right index finger to open up the loop and pull it taut, then release it to straighten out the dreadlock.

# Instructions
Hat is knit in the round from the brim to the crown. Switch to double-pointed needles during crown decreases when the stitches no longer reach around the circular needle.

## Ribbing
With B and smaller circular needles, cast on 64 (68, 76) sts, work in k2, p2 ribbing for 4 rows. Join to work in the round, placing marker at end of round.

Switch to C and work in ribbing for 1 round, then work 1 round of ribbing with B.

**Rep last 2 rounds** 1 (1, 2) more times, then continue with B only for 4 (4, 6) rounds, stranding C along wrong side of work. With C, work 2 (4, 4) rounds of ribbing, then work 2 rounds of ribbing with B. Ribbing measures approx 2 1/2, (3, 3 1/2)"/6.5 (7.5, 9)cm.

## Crown
With A and larger needles, k 1 round, inc 1 (inc 2, dec 1) sts evenly around—65 (70, 75) sts.

**Next round:** With B k1 (2, 3) sts, (make one 2.5"/6.5cm dreadlock into next st, k3) rep around hat.

Work in St st in A for 4 rounds, stranding B and C up along inside of hat by twisting with strand of A every other round.

**Next round:** (With C k3, then make one 3"/7.5cm dreadlock in next st) rep to end of round, end k1 (2, 3) sts.

Work in St st in A for 4 rounds, stranding B and C up along inside of hat by twisting with strand of A every other round.

**Next round:** (With B, make one 4"/10cm dreadlock, k1 with C, k1 with B, with C make one 4"/10cm dreadlock, k1 with B, k1 with C), rep to end of round, end k5 (4, 3) sts, alternating sts in B and C as established. Cut A, leaving a 6"/15cm tail.

Work in St st in A for 4 rounds, stranding B up along inside of hat by twisting with strand of A every other round.

**Next round:** (With B, make one 4.5"/11.5cm dreadlock, k1 with A, k1 with B, with A make one 4.5"/11.5cm dreadlock, k1 with B, k1 with A), rep to end of round, end k5 (4, 3) sts, alternating sts in A and B as est.

## Crown Shaping

Change to dpns when sts no longer fit on circ.

**Next round:** With A, (k3, k2tog) 13 (14, 15) times around all sts—52 (56, 60) sts rem.

Work 3 rounds in A with no decreasing.

**Next round:** (With A k1, then make one 5"/12.5cm dreadlock in next st) rep to end of round.

**Next round:** With A, (k2, k2tog) 13 (14, 15) times around all sts—39 (42, 45) sts rem.

Work 2 rounds in A with no decreasing.

**Next round:** (With A k1, then make one 5"/12.5cm dreadlock in next st), rep to end of round. End k1 (0, 1).

**Next round:** With A, (k1, k2tog) 13 (14, 15) times around all sts - 26 (28, 30) sts rem.

Work 1 round in A with no decreasing.

**Next round:** (With A k1, then with A and C held together make one 3"/7.5cm dreadlock) rep to end of round.

**Next round:** With A, k2tog around—13 (14, 15) sts rem.

Work 1 round in A with no decreasing.

**Next round:** (With A k1, then with A and C held together make one 3"/7.5cm dreadlock), rep around all sts, end k1 (0, 1). Cut B, leaving a 6"/15cm tail.

**Next round:** With A, k2tog around, end k1 (0,1)—7 (7, 8) sts rem.

**Next round:** With A, k all sts.

Cut A, leaving a 9"/23cm tail, draw tail through rem sts and pull tightly.

## Finishing

Block piece, Weave in all ends, use B tail at start of work to sew first 2 rows of ribbing together. With a strand of B, tie all A/B dreadlocks from the last round together to form a pigtail at the tip of the hat.

## This hat was knit with:

Classic Elite's, *Temptation*, 110yd/100m, 3.5 oz/100g per skein
(A) 2 balls, color HAGI-30 Red
(B) 2 balls, color HAGI-15 Black
(C) 1 ball, color HAGI-01 White

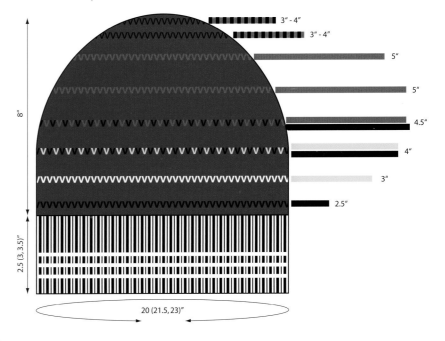

**SKILL LEVEL**
Easy

**FINISHED
MEASUREMENTS**
**Girth:** 9.5 (12.5, 15.5, 18.5,
21, 25.5, 28.5, 31.5)"/24 (32,
39.5, 47, 53.5, 65, 72.5, 80)cm
*See Dog Sizes on page
20 for tips on choosing the
correct size.*

# Rasta Dog Jacket

Why should Fido miss out on the fun? The body of this jacket is
knit in easy stripes, the chest is shaped with ribbing, and the collar
is decorated with doggie dreadlocks so your dog can pretend he's
a wild beast…way cool, man.

## MATERIALS

**Approx total:** 243 (304, 380,
456, 547, 656, 788, 946)yd/221
(277, 346, 415, 498, 597, 717,
861)m chunky weight
wool/llama blend yarn

**Color A:** 102 (128, 160, 192,
230, 276, 332, 398)yd/93 (116,
146, 175, 209, 251, 302,
362)m in red

**Color B:** 77 (96, 120, 144,
173, 207, 249, 299)yd/70 (87,
109, 131, 157, 188, 227,
272)m in black

**Color C:** 64 (80, 100, 120,
144, 173, 207, 249)yd/58 (73,
91, 109, 131, 157, 188, 227)m
in natural

4 sts and 6 rows = 1"/2.5cm
in St st

*Always take time to check
your gauge.*

**Knitting needles**
5.5mm (Size 9 U.S.)
*or size to obtain gauge*

5mm (Size H-8 U.S.)
crochet hook

Hook-and-loop fastener tape,
7.75 (10.5, 13.5, 16.5, 19.25,
22.25, 25, 28)"/19.5 (26.5, 34.5,
42, 49, 56.5, 63.5, 71)cm piece

## Special Pattern Stitch
### MAKE DREADLOCK (MD)
Knit into next stitch, but do not slide stitch off of the left-hand needle. With your right index finger, pull the new loop off of the right-hand needle and toward you, making total length of loop twice the length from needle to your right hand as desired for finished dreadlock. Twist loop clockwise until it is very tight, then slip loop off of right index finger onto LH needle, allowing loop to twist onto itself. Knit loop together with same stitch it came out of. If necessary, use your right index finger to open up the loop and pull it taut, then release it to even out the dreadlock twist.

# Instructions
Sweater is knit flat in one piece. Dreadlocks are worked around the collar, and a row of single crochet finishes the edging.

## Body
With a strand of A, cast on 18 (26, 34, 38, 46, 50, 58, 66) sts.

Knit 2 rows.

**Next row (RS):** K2, place marker (pm), k to last 2 sts, pm, k2.

**Next row (WS):** K2, slip marker (sm), M1, p to next marker, sm, k2.

**Next row (RS):** K2, sm, M1, k to next marker, sm, k2.

**Rep last 2 rows** until there are 38 (50, 62, 74, 86, 102, 114, 126) sts.

## CONTRASTING STRIPES

**Next row (RS):** With B, k2, sm, k to end of row, sm, k2.

**Next row (WS):** K2, sm, p to end of row, sm, k2.

**Rep last two rows twice,** then work 2 rows in same manner with A. Repeat last 6 rows with no increasing until piece measures 4.75 (6.5, 8.25, 10.25, 12, 13.75, 15.5, 17.25)"/12 (16.5, 21, 26, 30.5, 35, 39, 44)cm from cast-on row. End with a WS row. Break A.

## ARMHOLE SHAPING DECREASE

**Next row (RS):** With B, BO 9 (10, 14, 16, 19, 23, 24, 28) sts from start of next 2 rows, then BO 1 st at start of next 2 (4, 4, 4, 6, 6, 8, 8) rows—18 (26, 30, 38, 42, 50, 58, 62) sts.

## BEGIN RIBBING WITH B AND C

**Next row (RS):** With B, (k2, p2) to last 2 sts, end k2.

**Next row (WS):** K2, (k2, p2) to last 2 sts, end k2.

**Rep last 2 rows** with C. Cont working k2, p2 ribbing with edge sts worked in Garter Stitch (knit the first 2 and last 2 sts of every row), alternating colors B and C every two rows for a total of 1 (0, 3, 6, 7, 10, 8, 11) rows from start of ribbing.

## ARMHOLE SHAPING INCREASE

Cont ribbing with B and C est, inc 1 st at start of next 2 (4, 4, 4, 6, 6, 8, 8) rows, then cast on 5 (5, 7, 8, 10, 12, 12, 14)sts at start of next 2 rows—30 (40, 48, 58, 68, 80, 90, 98) sts.

## SHOULDER SHAPING

Cont in ribbing, dec 1 st at start of next 8 (10, 10, 12, 14, 18, 20, 20) rows—22 (30, 38, 46, 54, 62, 70, 78) sts, then BO 1 (1, 2, 2, 3, 3, 4, 4) sts at start of next 2 rows, then BO 1 (1, 2, 2, 3, 3, 4, 4) sts at start of next 2 rows—18 (26, 30, 38, 42, 50, 54, 62) sts rem.

# Dreadlock Collar

**Note:** In this section dreadlocks will be worked. Make the finished dreadlock between 2 and 4"/5 and 10 cm long, alternating the size of the locks to give a wild appearance. To add depth and variety, make a few of the dreadlocks with 2 strands of different colored yarn held together—be creative!

**Next row (RS):** With A, k0 (2, 0, 2, 0, 2, 0), (MD with A in next st, with C k2, MD with A and C held together in next st, with A k2) rep to end of row.

**Next row (WS):** Holding yarn to the public side of the work, (with A, k1, with C, k1) rep to end of row, making sure to twist strands of yarn in same direction for each stitch. Break C.

**Next row (RS):** With B, k1 (MD with B in next st, with A k2, MD with A and B held together in next st, with B k2) rep to end of row.

**Next row (WS):** Holding yarn to the public side of the work, (with A, k1, with B, k1) rep to end of row, making sure to twist strands of yarn in same direction for each stitch. Break A.

With B, work 2 rows of Garter Stitch. Bind off all sts loosely.

## Finishing

Block piece. With B, work 1 row of single crochet around entire edge of garment. Fit garment to dog, determining placement of hook-and-loop fastener when jacket is closed at stomach and front neck. Place fastener so the loop portion is on the underside of right edge and the hook portion of fastener to outside of left edge. Hand or machine-sew loop side of fastener to piece.

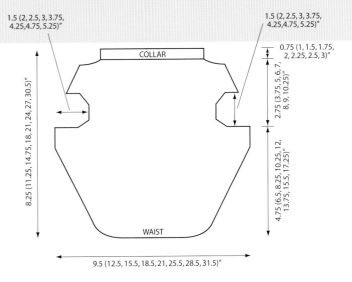

1.5 (2, 2.5, 3, 3.75, 4.25, 4.75, 5.25)"

1.5 (2, 2.5, 3, 3.75, 4.25, 4.75, 5.25)"

COLLAR

0.75 (1, 1.5, 1.75, 2, 2.25, 2.5, 3)"

8.25 (11.25, 14.75, 18, 21, 24, 27, 30.5)"

2.75 (3.75, 5, 6, 7, 8, 9, 10.25)"

4.75 (6.5, 8.25, 10.25, 12, 13.75, 15.5, 17.25)"

WAIST

9.5 (12.5, 15.5, 18.5, 21, 25.5, 28.5, 31.5)"

## This sweater was knit with:

Classic Elite's *Montera*, 50% llama/50% wool, 127yd/116m, 3.5oz/100g per skein

(A) 1 (2, 2, 2, 2, 3, 3, 3) skeins, color 3858 Cintachi Red
(B) 1 (1, 1, 2, 2, 2, 3, 3) skeins, color 3813 Black
(C) 1 (1, 1, 1, 2, 2, 2, 2) skeins, color 3816 Lapaz Natural

MEN WHO KNIT

### Andres Nevarez
San Francisco, California

"I feel an earth-connection when I knit, thinking that I'm doing something that my ancestors have done throughout the years."

# Fluffy Handpaint Dog Bed

If you have a pampered pooch, this furry bed will be a welcome addition to his or her collection of comfortable and fashionable home accents. Made with bouclé and faux fur yarn, it couldn't be more posh. Starting in the center of the circle with just four stitches, you increase every fourth row until the bed is the desired size.

## MATERIALS
**Approx total:** 900 (1200, 1440)yd/819 (1092, 1310)m bulky boucle and faux fur yarn

**Yarn A:** 500 (700, 840)yd/455 (637, 764)m of acrylic/polyester bulky boucle yarn in variegated browns and greens

**Yarn B:** 400 (500, 600)yd/364 (455, 546)m of polyester faux fur yarn in olive

**Knitting needles**
4mm (Size 6 U.S.) double-pointed needles and circular needles in 12"/30.5cm, 24"/61cm and 36"/91.5cm lengths *or size to obtain gauge*

Machine washable polyester fiberfill, 24 to 36oz/672g to 1kg

20 stitch markers (1 in a contrasting color)

Darning needle for sewing seams and weaving in ends

## GAUGE
4 1/2 sts and 6 1/4 rows = 1"/2.5 cm in St st

*Always take time to check your gauge.*

## Special Pattern Stitch
**I-CORD HORIZONTAL STRIPE**
(CO 1 st using Cable CO, keep new st on right-hand needle. K2, k2tog-LS. Sl 3 sts from right-hand needle back onto left-hand needle), repeat across work until all sts are worked.

# Instructions

Eyelash yarn can be annoying, there's no escaping that. The same property that makes it such a cool fabric is also what makes it hard to handle—its furriness. If it's any consolation, once you get a few rounds into an eyelash yarn project it will seem much easier. Your hands will have the feel of the yarn and will automatically compensate for the odd feeling.

Be sure to count your stitches—it's easy to lose a stitch or two, only to discover this when a dropped stitch is apparent after the piece is finished. Stitch markers strategically placed to mark sections will make it easier to keep a constant count (and to discover where you may have lost a stitch, if that happens).

## Bed Bottom
With A, cast 4 sts onto a dpn.

**Next row:** (K1, m1) to end of row—8 sts.

**Next row:** M1, (k1, m1) to end of row—17 sts.

**Next row:** Knit all sts, dividing them around dpns, join to knit in the round.

**Knit 3 rounds** with no increasing, then inc in 4th round as follows:

**Next round:** (K and p into next st, place marker) to end of round—34 sts, 17 markers.

Cont inc in similar manner, working 3 rounds in St st with no inc, then inc 1 st after each marker every 4th round 12 (19, 26) more times until there are 221 (340, 459) sts—13 (20, 27) sts in each section.

When piece is large enough, move to 12"/30.5cm needle, then to 24"/61cm needle, and 36"/91.5cm needle. Your circle should be approx 16 (24, 32)"/40.5 (61, 81.5)cm across.

Inc 1 (0, 1) sts around all sts in last round—222 (340, 460) sts. End with a knit round, remove markers in last round, leaving 1 marker to note start of round.

## Bed Sides

Work I-Cord Horizontal Stripe around all sts as follows: (CO 1 st using Cable CO, keep new st on right-hand needle. K2, k2tog-LS. Slip 3 sts from right-hand needle back onto left-hand needle), repeat around until all sts are worked.

**Next round:** (K2, p2) rep to end of round. Cont in k2, p2 ribbing for 6"/15cm.

**Next round:** Work I-Cord Horizontal Stripe around all sts.

**Next round:** Knit all sts, dec 1 (0, 1) st in round and replacing markers every 13 (20, 27) sts to create 17 equal sections.

## Bed Top

With 2 strands of B held together, knit all sts. Dec 1 st after each marker every 4th round until 85 sts rem on needle.

Change to shorter circ and dpns as necessary.

## Stuffing Bed

At this point, stop knitting and weave in loose ends. Stuff dog bed with fiberfill, leaving enough room at top to continue knitting comfortably. Do not overfill! Cont dec until 17 sts rem.

**Next round:** Remove markers, (k7, k2tog), rep until 8 sts rem. Break yarn, leaving a 9"/22cm tail.

## Finishing

With darning needle, draw tail through 8 rem sts. Tie off and weave in end.

**This bed was knit with:**
(A) 3 (3, 4) balls of Lion Brand Yarn's *Homespun*, 98% acrylic, 2% polyester, 185yd/168m, 6oz/170g per skein, color 335 Prairie
(B) 7 (8, 10) balls of Lion Brand Yarn's *Fun Fur*, 100% polyester, 60 yd/55m, 1.75oz/50g per ball, color 132 Olive

MEN WHO KNIT

## Michael Cook
Dallas, Texas

"Needless to say, since I raise silkworms and reel the silk from their cocoons, silk is my favorite yarn to knit with."

# Sample & Test Knitters

*Men's Raglan Mock Soy Silk Turtleneck* by Lou Simon

*Variegated Yoke Pullover* by Paulette Rand

*Men's Knit Zip Front Pullover* by Scott Simpson

*Shades of Gray Sweater* by Carol Didier

*Boy Toy,* test knit by Adina Alexander, Cathi Arfin, Tanya Brooks,
 Craig Rosenfeld, Jon Thumin, Martin Webster, Martha Weninger

*Garter & Stripe Pullover* by Kathleen Catlett

*Pet Box Sofa* by Grumperina

*Plaid Zip Front Jacket* by Melissa Morgan-Oakes

*Cotton Cabled Pullover with Color* by Laura Messina

*Faupi Lopi Cardigan* by Judy Seip

*Mitered Dog Blanket* by Lawrence Joseph

*Diagonal Colorblock Pullover* by Doug Iberg

*Garter Rib Scarf and Hat* by Brian Blaho

*Double Roll-Neck Simple Sweater* by Drew Emborsky, test knit by
 Kenny Chua and Ami Brabson

*Man's Dreadlock Hat,* test knit by Daniel Thorton

*Rasta Dog Jacket,* test knit by Cheryl Kemp

*Fluffy Handpaint Dog Bed* by Julie Sparks

# Metric Chart

| INCHES | METRIC (MM/CM) | INCHES | METRIC (MM/CM) | INCHES | METRIC (MM/CM) |
|---|---|---|---|---|---|
| $1/8$ | 3 mm | $8^1/_2$ | 21.6 cm | 23 | 58.4 cm |
| $3/16$ | 5 mm | 9 | 22.9 cm | $23^1/_2$ | 59.7 cm |
| $1/4$ | 6 mm | $9^1/_2$ | 24.1 cm | 24 | 61 cm |
| $5/16$ | 8 mm | 10 | 25.4 cm | $24^1/_2$ | 62.2 cm |
| $3/8$ | 9.5 mm | $10^1/_2$ | 26.7 cm | 25 | 63.5 cm |
| $7/16$ | 1.1 cm | 11 | 27.9 cm | $25^1/_2$ | 64.8 cm |
| $1/2$ | 1.3 cm | $11^1/_2$ | 29.2 cm | 26 | 66 cm |
| $9/16$ | 1.4 cm | 12 | 30.5 cm | $26^1/_2$ | 67.3 cm |
| $5/8$ | 1.6 cm | $12^1/_2$ | 31.8 cm | 27 | 68.6 cm |
| $11/16$ | 1.7 cm | 13 | 33 cm | $27^1/_2$ | 69.9 cm |
| $3/4$ | 1.9 cm | $13^1/_2$ | 34.3 cm | 28 | 71.1 cm |
| $13/16$ | 2.1 cm | 14 | 35.6 cm | $28^1/_2$ | 72.4 cm |
| $7/8$ | 2.2 cm | $14^1/_2$ | 36.8 cm | 29 | 73.7 cm |
| $15/16$ | 2.4 cm | 15 | 38.1 cm | $29^1/_2$ | 74.9 cm |
| 1 | 2.5 cm | $15^1/_2$ | 39.4 cm | 30 | 76.2 cm |
| $1^1/_2$ | 3.8 cm | 16 | 40.6 cm | $30^1/_2$ | 77.5 cm |
| 2 | 5 cm | $16^1/_2$ | 41.9 cm | 31 | 78.7 cm |
| $2^1/_2$ | 6.4 cm | 17 | 43.2 cm | $31^1/_2$ | 80 cm |
| 3 | 7.6 cm | $17^1/_2$ | 44.5 cm | 32 | 81.3 cm |
| $3^1/_2$ | 8.9 cm | 18 | 45.7 cm | $32^1/_2$ | 82.6 cm |
| 4 | 10.2 cm | $18^1/_2$ | 47 cm | 33 | 83.8 cm |
| $4^1/_2$ | 11.4 cm | 19 | 48.3 cm | $33^1/_2$ | 85 cm |
| 5 | 12.7 cm | $19^1/_2$ | 49.5 cm | 34 | 86.4 cm |
| $5^1/_2$ | 14 cm | 20 | 50.8 cm | $34^1/_2$ | 87.6 cm |
| 6 | 15.2 cm | $20^1/_2$ | 52 cm | 35 | 88.9 cm |
| $6^1/_2$ | 16.5 cm | 21 | 53.3 cm | $35^1/_2$ | 90.2 cm |
| 7 | 17.8 cm | $21^1/_2$ | 54.6 cm | 36 | 91.4 cm |
| $7^1/_2$ | 19 cm | 22 | 55 cm | $36^1/_2$ | 92.7 cm |
| 8 | 20.3 cm | $22^1/_2$ | 57.2 cm | 37 | 94.0 cm |

# Acknowledgments

There are many, many folks whose hard work and imagination make a book possible, and this book is no exception!

I would like to thank the staff at Lark Books who worked so hard to make this such a beautiful book—especially Deborah, whose initial enthusiasm carried me over many rough spots. I could not have worked through these patterns without the help of Donna, my tech editor, and I found a constant source of inspiration and laughter in my co-author, Drew— thanks so much to both of you! Thanks to my agent Bob, for helping me maneuver through the publishing world with such cheerfulness, and big thanks to Keith Wright for taking such lovely photographs, and to Orrin Lundgren for his excellent illustrations.

I'd also like to thank every knitter who worked up a sample or test garment for me. We weren't able to use every item knitted, but everything that was worked up helped us to gain a greater understanding of how to make the patterns as clear as possible. (A complete list of the sample and test knitters who contributed to this book can be found on page 141.)

I'd love to give a hug and a scratch on the belly to all of the male and canine models (respectively). You all wear a sweater wonderfully and make me very proud!

The yarn companies who helped out by providing yarn for swatching and sampling were lifesavers, and I thank each and every one from the bottom of my heart for their trust in allowing me to use their lovely fibers.

And finally, I thank my family—Hannah, Max, and Gerry—without whom this book would not have been possible, and wouldn't have meant as much. I take great pride in my knitting kids; my exceptional knitting daughter, and my own personal **little man who knits.**

# Author Bios

Annie Modesitt learned to knit at age 25 and promptly went to work for *Vogue Knitting*. The job didn't stick but the knitting did, and she was hooked for life. After a 10-year hiatus from designing knitwear, she returned to the needles and yarn in 2000 after the birth of her last child.

Annie prefers to knit using the Combination style, but feels that every knitter must find the style that suits him or her best. Aside from knitting and designing, Annie teaches knit and crochet skills throughout North America, and writes about fiber arts. Her designs have appeared in *Interweave Knits*, *Vogue Knitting*, *Knitters*, *Interweave Crochet*, *Cast On*, and many other fiber-related periodicals.

Annie is the author of *Confessions of a Knitting Heretic*, *Knitting Millinery* (ModeKnit Press, Apr. 2003 and Sept. 2004), *Twist & Loop* (Potter Craft, Oct. 2006), and is the editor of the 2006 and 2007 *Crochet Pattern A Day Calendar* (Accord Publishing), and *Cheaper Than Therapy, Joy, Healing & Life Lessons in Fiber* (ModeKnit Press, Sept. 2005). She is currently working on a collection of hand knits inspired by vintage shaping techniques, *Romantic Knits* (due out summer 2007 from Potter Craft). Visit her website at www.anniemodesitt.com.

Drew Emborsky's quirky title as "The Crochet Dude" and his kitschy tongue-in-cheek designs have propelled him from anonymity as a fiber artist to recognition as a cutting edge fiber designer. His unique role as a male knitter and crocheter has opened doors for other men who were stuck in the closet with their yarn, knitting needles, and crochet hooks.

Drew studied fine art at Kendall College of Art & Design in Grand Rapids, Michigan, and is a national member of the Crochet Guild of America, where he received a master certificate in crochet. He has been featured in national publications including *BUST* Magazine, *Interweave Crochet*, and *Knit.1*, as well as international newspapers such as *The Sunday Telegraph* (London).

Emborsky launched his website and blog in February 2005, and has gained a loyal following throughout the world—his wildly popular blog receives thousands of visits per day. Visit it at www.thecrochetdude.blogspot.com to see what he is up to today and to find links to his line of crochet patterns. Drew lives in Houston, Texas, with his two cats, Chandler and Cleocatra.

# Index